Many Heavens, One Earth

Many Heavens, One Earth

Readings on Religion and the Environment

Edited by Clifford Chalmers Cain

LEXINGTON BOOKS
Lanham • Boulder • New York • Toronto • Plymouth, UK

Published by Lexington Books
A wholly owned subsidiary of The Rowman & Littlefield Publishing Group, Inc.
4501 Forbes Boulevard, Suite 200, Lanham, Maryland 20706
www.rowman.com

10 Thornbury Road, Plymouth PL6 7PP, United Kingdom

British Library Cataloguing in Publication Information Available

Library of Congress Cataloging-in-Publication Data
The hardback edition was previously cataloged by the Library of Congress as follows:

Many heavens, one earth : readings on religion and the environment / edited by Clifford
Chalmers Cain.
     p. cm.
   Includes index.
   1. Nature—Religious aspects. 2. Ecotheology. 3. Human ecology—Religious aspects.
I. Cain, Clifford C.
   BL65.N35M36 2012
   207'.77—dc23   2011044403

ISBN 978-0-7391-7295-7 (cloth : alk. paper)
ISBN 978-0-7391-8438-7 (pbk. : alk. paper)
ISBN 978-0-7391-7296-4 (electronic)

Printed in the United States of America

To my sister
Jan Castle
and
in memory of
Ethel Virginia Cain
Clifford Chalmers Cain, Sr.
Tony Castle
Virginia Duffey
Virgil McElyea
and
Kent Sexton
You remain in our hearts.

Contents

Foreword

For the last thirty-five years, Annie Dillard's *Pilgrim at Tinker Creek* has been a staple of environmental literature. The book is structured as a rite of passage (pilgrimage), and God language is woven deeply into it. As such, it celebrates Dillard's vision of the transcendence and sacredness of the natural world. But will we still be reading *Pilgrim* thirty-five years from now? Maybe not. Increasingly the issues which dominate public discussion of the environment— climate change and environmental justice, for example—do not foreground the conception of nature as sacred. On the contrary, a rhetoric of scientific, economic, and legal rationality is cutting a wider and wider swath across our discourse about the environment. If current trends continue, the likelihood of a loss of religious vocabulary about nature appears to be high.

Clifford Chalmers Cain and the other writers of the essays in this book are firmly convinced that a lexicon of spirituality is vital to the resolution of our current ecological crisis. To that end, their efforts collected here begin to expound the wisdom of the world's religious traditions with regard to nature and the environment. These writers understand the world religions as a rich source of narratives, symbols, and rituals through which to construct and maintain a healthy and sustainable relationship with the environment. In particular, the insights of religions are regarded here as powerful—and necessary—critiques of excessively secular perspectives on the natural world. At the heart of this book lies the conviction that our ecological crisis is (as Paul Brockelman puts it in his essay) "a spiritual crisis involving our moral and spiritual attitudes toward nature."

In that sense, these essays can be read as a collection of words from prophets. For each writer speaks as an intermediary between a specific religious tradition on the one hand and our ecological crisis on the other. Each essay connects something transcendent with something mundane, carrying a message (as Mircea Eliade would say) from the sacred to the profane. Like prophets, these writers have listened to the wisdom of their spiritual traditions, and as a result they know that the problems confronting us cannot fully be solved apart from those traditions. But that is not to say that this book captures only a chorus of voices crying in the wilderness. For these writers are not what scholars of religion call "peripheral prophets," i.e., advocates for change who are located at the margins of their society, far from centers of power. On the contrary, in recent years concern for the environment has moved into those centers, and the ecological crisis now occupies the attention of those who are at home in the corridors of economic, legal, scientific, and political power. In addition, leading intellectuals are increasingly concerned that secular rationalities are (in the words of Jürgen Habermas) "missing something." Like prophets, the voices in these pages call a society in peril back to spiritual resources that have been sidelined or forgotten, judged as obsolete or unnecessary, but which nevertheless offer the wisdom and guidance that is most needed in the hour of danger.

In thirty-five years, will the next generation be reading *Pilgrim at Tinker Creek*? Let's hope so. And let us also hope that they will still be listening to the wisdom of the prophets, especially as recorded here in *Many Heavens, One Earth*.

Byron R. McCane, Ph.D.
Albert C. Outler Professor of
Religion and Department Chair
Wofford College
Spartanburg, South Carolina

Preface

This collection of essays by fifteen scholars and adherents within nine various religious traditions from around the world may be read as a separate entity standing on its own or as an accompanying primary resource to *Down to Earth: Religious Paths toward Custodianship of Nature* (Rowman and Littlefield, 2009).

While the secondary analysis of world religions in *Down to Earth* attempts to be objective and balanced, and accents common threads among these religions, there are value and vibrancy in hearing from individual voices from within these traditions—faithful adherents and/or specialist scholars—voices which speak in a personal, connected, committed way from/about each of these spiritual moorings and which also resonate with the plethora of environmental problems which jeopardize the well-being and quality of life of religious and non-religious citizens of the globe.

Care has been taken to choose individuals whose scholarship and insights are apparent, compelling, and well-respected, both internally and externally to the specific traditions. While none of the contributors would claim or could claim to be representative of an entire individual religion's diversity, each person shares faithfully and forthrightly the resources which he or she believes that particular spiritual heritage brings to the environmental predicament which challenges world communities today—a situation resulting not only from the specific ecological problems faced, but also from the underlying diseases of consumerism, materialism, and greed from which the environmental symptoms emerge.

For their generosity in sharing their thoughts with others, and their willingness to have their work included in this volume, a deep debt of gratitude is owed to the contributors. For, indeed, if environmental challenges are to be successfully met, the rich resources of religion must be tapped: Religion's power to inform, guide, motivate, and enthuse must join science's power to observe, hypothesize, test, and theorize. Scientific knowledge and religious inspiration must combine forces in order to engage persons' heads and hearts in consciously and conscientiously addressing the ecological crisis which besets earth and threatens to leave an environmentally-impoverished planet to future generations.

Clifford Chalmers Cain
Jefferson City, Missouri
The Feast of Epiphany, 2012

Acknowledgments

Many thanks are extended to Samantha Kirk, previous Acquisitions Editor, for her helpful suggestions at the start of this project, and to Emily Natsios, Assistant Editor, Production, for going far beyond the call of duty in enabling it to come to fruition; to Byron McCane, longtime friend, archaeologist, and outstanding teacher at Wofford College, for the Foreword; to Charlene Hawkins, artist *extraordinaire* and new friend, for permission to use her painting "Tree of Life" on the book's cover; to Perry Kea, friend and cutting-edge biblical scholar at the University of Indianapolis, and to Marti Steussy, fellow theologian and creative spirit at Christian Theological Seminary, for their reviews and reflections; to Vicki Mast, technology expert and friend, for surmounting innumerable computer obstacles and challenges; to Samantha ("Samm") Quinn, college student, for her tireless data entry; to Gina Campagna, Assistant Director of Advancement Services at Westminster College, for the author's photograph; and especially to my wife Dr. Natasia Sexton Cain, children Rachel and Zachary, and granddaughter Madison, for their love and support.

Grateful appreciation is expressed for permission to reprint the following articles:

To University Press of New England for Paul Brockelman, "With New Eyes: Seeing the Environment as a Spiritual Issue," from *The Greening of Faith*, chapter 2, edited by John Carroll, Paul Brockelman, and Mary Westfall, copyright 1997.

To Associated University Presses for Eric Katz, "Judaism and the Ecological Crisis," and for Mary Evelyn Tucker, "Ecological Themes in Taoism and Confucianism," from *Worldviews and Ecology*, edited by Mary Evelyn Tucker and John A. Grim, pp. 55-70 and pp. 150-160, copyright 1994.

To *Crux* journal for Iain Provan, "The Land Is Mine and You Are Only Tenants," from Vol. 42, No. 2 (Summer, 2006), pp. 3-16, copyright 2006.

To the American Baptist Historical Society for Clifford Chalmers Cain, "Stewardship as a Work of Art," from *The American Baptist Quarterly*, Vol. XVII, No. 1 (March, 1998), pp. 59-69, copyright 1998.

To Elizabeth Theokritoff for "The Orthodox Church and the Environmental Movement," revised version, copyright 2008, first published in *Orthodoxy and Ecology Resource Book*, edited by Alexander Belopopsky and Dimitri Oikonomou, copyright 1996.

To Oxford University Press for Seyyed Hossein Nasr, "Religion and the Resacralization of Nature," from *Religion and the Order of Nature*, by Seyyed Hossein Nasr, pp. 270-292, copyright 1996, and for Joel Martin, "Circling Earth," from *The Land Looks After Us*, by Joel Martin, pp. 5-29, copyright 1999.

To University of Washington Press which specified that the letter/speech attributed to Chief Seattle resides in the public domain.

To Prentice Hall/Pearson Education for David Kingsley, "Native American Religion: Ecological Themes," from *Ecology and Religion*, by David Kingsley, pp. 42-50, copyright 1995.

To Springer-Verlag for Christopher Key Chapple, "Ecological Non-violence and the Hindu Tradition," from *Perspectives on Non-violence*, edited by V.K. Kool, pp. 168-177, copyright 1990.

To Beacon Press for His Holiness the Fourteenth Dalai Lama, "A Tibetan Buddhist Perspective on Spirit in Nature," from *Spirit and Nature*, edited by Steven C. Rockefeller and John C. Elder, pp. 110-123, copyright 1992.

To Susan M. Darlington for "Rethinking Buddhism and Development: The Emergence of Environmentalist Monks in Thailand," from *Journal of Buddhist Ethics*, Vol. 7 (2000), copyright 2000.

To Gopinder Kaur Sagoo for "Our Environment and Us: A Sikh Perspective," first published in *World Religions in Education—The Environment*, Shap Working Party, UK (2008/2009), copyright 2009.

To Sikhspectrum.com for S. Lourdunathan, "Ecosophical Concerns in the Sikh Tradition," first published in *The Sikh Review* (2002), copyright 2002.

Introduction to article by Paul Brockelman

Environmental problems are, at their root, spiritual issues: That is, they result from the exploitation and degradation of nature prompted and sanctioned by greed, "growthism," progress, and consumerism. Indeed, humans have been seduced by the "consumer values system," and as a result, are "slaves of [their] consumer needs." Consequently, if these problems are going to be solved, they will require a spiritual reorientation that advocates and legitimates caring, service, and protection. That reorientation—plus the knowledge provided by science—will go a long way toward successfully addressing ecological challenges.

In this article, religion professor Paul Brockelman stresses that the way we see nature will determine the way we fit-in to it. Drawing from the experience of naturalist John Muir (who came to see nature as "God's holy creation"), he posits a re-visioning of nature through "the amazed eyes of a child" in which human beings belong to a "broader, sacred reality and community," and in which humans connect to a kinship among all living beings. Thus, humans need a broader or bigger vision of reality in which they see and understand themselves as part of a greater whole which is interconnected and interdependent. Therefore, nature is not a commodity to be owned, abused, and misused; rather, it is a community to be loved and reverenced.

With New Eyes:
Seeing the Environment as a Spiritual Issue

Paul Brockelman

In the last analysis, the psychological roots of the crisis humanity is facing on a global scale seem to lie in the loss of the spiritual perspective. Since a harmonious experience of life requires, among other things, fulfillment of transcendent needs, a culture that has denied spirituality and has lost access to the transpersonal dimension of existence is doomed to failure in all other avenues of its activities.

Stanislav Groff

Revisioning Life

Like many young men in their twenties, John Muir, who was later to become famous as a naturalist and conservationist, went through a period of profound turmoil and disorientation in which he struggled to find himself and his role in life. Pulled this way and that, he couldn't seem to discover who he was or was to become. Although he was "touched with melancholy and loneliness . . . and the pressure of time upon life," he was unable to settle upon a direction for his life and remained disoriented and mired in indecision.

It wasn't until an accident occurred to him in March, 1868, that he was able to launch himself upon his career as a wilderness explorer. In a factory in which he manufactured agricultural implements of his own invention, a belt on one of the machines flew up and pierced his right eye on the edge of the cornea. He was blinded in that eye, and his left eye soon became blinded through nerve shock and sympathy. He was left in utter darkness. Unable to see, he tells us, "I would gladly have died. . . . My eyes closed forever on all God's beauty! . . . I am lost!"

After careful examination, however, a specialist indicated that he would eventually see again, imperfectly in the right eye but normally in the left. What he needed to do was to remain for a month in a darkened room. He did that, all the while dreaming of wilderness such as Yosemite Valley in the Sierras. Finally, on an April day a little over a month after the accident, the remaining bandages were removed from his eyes and the shades from the windows. Beyond all hope and happiness, he was able to see the world again! He was, in fact, intoxicated by that resurrection of his sight. It was as if he were seeing everything anew, with new eyes as it were, fresh from the hand of God. The experience transformed him. With the awareness that he could find no happiness apart from wild nature and "that I might be true to myself," he reoriented his life to exploring that nature and advocating its conservation. "The affliction has driven me to the sweet fields," he said. "God has to nearly kill us sometimes to teach us lessons."[1] It was from this time that his continuous wanderings began. As he put it, "I bade adieu to all my mechanical inventions, determined to devote the rest of my life to the study of the inventions of God."[2]

The British philosopher John Wisdom tells an interesting story about religious knowledge or belief in a classic essay titled, "Gods." It is a story that might help us better understand Muir's experience. Two friends, one a theist and one an atheist, return to a long-neglected garden of theirs. Weeds have sprouted up since they left, but in-between the weeds they find a few of the old plants still surprisingly vigorous. Having inspected the entire garden, the theist comes to the conclusion that an invisible gardener has been taking care of it, whereas his atheist friend concludes that there has been no invisible gardener. Both agree about all the facts: Gardens need sunlight, water, fertile soil, and so on. In fact, we can even imagine that the friends carry out a thorough study to ascertain all the facts that might influence and determine any possible garden, and they reach total agreement about them. Thus, Wisdom seems to be saying, their varying beliefs concerning the existence of an invisible gardener who tends the garden is simply not a factual or empirical hypothesis that can be demonstrated experimentally. It would seem, then, that both the theist's belief in an invisible gardener and his atheist friend's contradictory belief that there is no such gardener are more like ways of "seeing" the garden as a meaningful whole than like empirical hypotheses that are confirmed or disconfirmed by any possible facts concerning gardens.[3]

In this sense, spiritual understanding is more like suddenly seeing the famous *gestalt* figure [such as ink blots that defy absolute interpretation and thus allow for a breadth of understanding] meaningfully either as a vase or as two faces than like constructing an empirical hypothesis or a deductive syllogism. Religious faith and insight provide an overarching interpretive understanding of life as a *meaningful* whole, including our own role and destiny within it.[4]

John Muir's experience, then, was a religious revisioning, a revisioning that transformed not only how he saw nature, but also how he envisaged his role within it as a naturalist and conservationist. As we have seen, he changed how he lived because of it.

Pushed by the stultifying and painful spiritual condition in which he had been living and transformed by the shock of his temporary blindness, Muir came to see nature with the amazed eyes of a child again and to understand his own role within it in a new way. In his early essay, "Nature," Ralph Waldo Emerson had described such a transforming vision this way: "Few adults can see nature. Most persons do not see the sun. At least they have a very superficial seeing. The sun illuminates only the eye of the man, but shines into the eye and the heart of the child."[5] Muir's wonder at the extraordinary miracle of life, at the incredible epiphany it manifested, touched him to his core and enabled him to find his authentic orientation in life. In traditional religious terminology, he became spiritually reoriented because he discovered his own connection to a broader, sacred reality and community to which he belonged, a reality that permitted him to see how he might live more deeply and meaningfully than hitherto. He put it this way in his journals:

> The man of science, the naturalist, too often loses sight of the essential oneness of all living beings in seeking to classify them in kingdoms, orders, families, genera, species, etc., taking note of the kind and arrangement of limbs, teeth, toes, scales, hair, feathers, etc., measured and set forth in meters, centimeters, and millimeters, while the eye of the Poet, the Seer, never closes on the kinship of all God's creatures, and his heart ever beats in sympathy with great and small alike as "earth-born companions and fellow mortals" equally dependent on Heaven's eternal love.[6]

His spiritual transformation, then, wasn't so much a shift in how he thought about things, as a shift in how he looked at them, how he felt about them, and how he actually acted and behaved toward them. He found his way in life by finding his way home to nature.

All of us at various times have touched the spiritual and moral condition at a deep level of seriousness. Perhaps it happened during a divorce, the death of a parent, hitting bottom after a serious addiction, the loss of a job on which one depended financially or emotionally, the outbreak of war, or some other trauma that led to a disintegration of one's familiar and everyday way of seeing things.

Such spiritual reorientations as that of Muir, of course, are not limited to individuals alone. Historians and scholars of various kinds have long been aware that human cultures also occasionally undergo such transformations in how they envisage life as a meaningful whole and how they picture the purpose and role of humans within it. To find examples of such paradigm shifts in the fundamental world of our own culture we would have to go back to the cultural revolution constituted by the replacement of fertility goddesses with male warrior gods after 2500 B.C.E.; the shift from polytheism to "radical monotheism" (to use H. Richard Niebuhr's trenchant phrase) in early Jewish history; the change to Christianity in fourth- and fifth-century Rome; and the startling transformation of the by-then traditional European Christian culture into what we now call "modernity" or "the modern world" in the seventeenth, eighteenth, and nineteenth centuries.

In the face of the ecological difficulties avalanching down upon us, it may be that all of us, like Muir, will be forced to reevaluate how we "see" nature and change our behavior toward it. Many observers of our contemporary world, in fact, argue just that and that such a reflective reevaluation and reorientation of our lives will entail a digging down to the foundations of our ultimate faith in life. In other words, getting our ecological bearings may first entail getting our spiritual bearings in life by finding our way back to our home in nature.

A Bird's-eye View of our Ecological Situation

It is probably safe to say that the present environmental state of the world constitutes the most serious threat to the biosphere since the origin of life on earth. It is also safe to say that the environmental crisis is not only a threat, but also a situation that will not be easily overcome and that will haunt us for the foreseeable future. In the words of the late Pope John Paul II, "our problems are the world's problems and burdens for generations to come."

Indeed, the all-too-familiar phrase, "ecological crisis," may be too feeble a way to put it. It is becoming increasingly clear to a number of observers that this is a crisis of the whole life system of the modern industrial world, one that affects both nature and the human culture it supports and sustains. Indeed, we seem to be living in a time in which we are witnessing not only breakdowns in the natural systems of the biosphere into which we have intruded with our economic and technological "progress," but also breakdowns in important parts of those economic, political, and cultural systems themselves. It seems increasingly clear that the familiar model of reality that hierarchically separates the human from the rest of life, or human cultures from nature, is both false and destructive of that wider nature.

In fact, contemporary science clearly shows that everything that has emerged on earth has emerged from and within nature as a whole. From this point of view, the economic, social, moral, and spiritual decay that is often manifested in our present world is not something that lies "outside" nature but is a biocultural development "within" it. Such cultural decay, then, is just one more manifestation of ecological disturbances and difficulties introduced by the modern industrial world. With all its obvious benefits, that modern industrial society that has so devastated our natural environment seems increasingly to be devastating us as well.[7] Putting the same thing another way, it would seem that to the degree that we have lost our sense of being rooted in a deeper and more encompassing natural order or reality, we have become spiritually, morally, and ecologically disoriented.

It would seem, then, that the avalanche of environmental issues we are currently witnessing around the globe calls for long-term consideration of how we are living and how that affects both the environment and ourselves rather than merely short-term technological "fixes." And yet, such long-term consideration is difficult for all of us precisely because we are so caught up in the pursuit of short-term economic and political "success." As Harvard theologian Gordon Kaufman has put it, "The organization of human economic life into institutions geared to satisfying human needs and wants . . . and of political life into nation-states, prevents us from directing our concerns and energies toward the larger world beyond our human-centered interests, and working for the common good of all creatures."[8]

Yes, But Is the Environment a Spiritual Issue?

Although certainly in part economic, demographic, and political in nature, the earth's ecological deterioration is at heart a matter of human attitudes toward the earth and life in general, attitudes that, of course, affect how we behave toward it. Thus, it would seem to constitute a spiritual crisis involving our moral and spiritual attitudes toward nature and, in fact, life as a whole. It may call for spiritual reflection on what we consider to be of ultimate importance in our lives and how we think we ought to live in light of that and moral reflection on how we understand and relate to nature.

But why? Is nature and our behavior toward it in any way a spiritual question? And why is it that the environment, which previously had rarely been thought to be such a spiritual issue, has in fact suddenly become so for increasing numbers of persons today? I think there are basically four reasons for this remarkable shift:

First of all, there is increasing recognition that a spiritual attitude toward nature has contributed to the increasingly dangerous environmental destruction and collapse we now see all around us. Newton, of course, thought of nature as an intricate machine fashioned by a designer God but running on its own according to the laws of mechanics. Since then, due to the ensuing industrial revolution, we seem to have totally commodified nature. We conceive of it as mere stuff stripped of any intrinsic value before it is forcibly extracted from the "wild" (meaning uncontrolled) and brought into the human economy—a "natural resource," as we put it, ready to be transformed industrially into useful products to improve the human condition. Aldo Leopold put it this way in his *Sand County Almanac*: "We abuse land because we regard it as a commodity belonging to us. When we see land as a community to which we belong, we may begin to use it with love and respect."[9]

Far from being a scientific or neutral hypothesis, this view of nature as a commodity put here simply for our use is itself an interpretive understanding, a way of seeing nature in much the same sense that John Wisdom's atheist (as well as the theist) brings a point-of-view to the garden beyond factual hypothesis. It is, then, a perspective on nature and life itself, a spiritual vision (if one can use that term for a point-of-view that denies the possibility of "spiritual" perspective at all), which of course is (or ought to be) quite different than, for example, a Jewish or Christian or Buddhist perspective. Many believe that a root cause of our violent destruction and transformation of nature lies in just such a modern perspective, which strips nature of any intrinsic value, not to mention epiphany [a manifestation of sacred presence]. It hardly seems possible that without that modern way of seeing it, we could have violated nature in quite the way we have and to the extent that we have. In this sense, then, the environment would seem to be unavoidably a spiritual issue.

But second, connected to (or perhaps embracing) this materialistic view of nature is a materialistic conception of "the good life." This is a thin vision of life as a whole that has flowered in modern times, a vision suggesting that the central thrust and significance of our lives consists of the accumulation of capital or material goods. As the bumper sticker puts it, "Whoever has the most things when he dies, wins!" It is almost as if the accumulation of goods and the kind of intensive attention their production and consumption entails shields us from death, as indeed it does seem to do to a certain degree.

This is a closed and mean conception of life, which not only thinks of nature as put here simply for our enjoyment, but anthropocentrically places human life at the center of everything (the entire universe!). Having accomplished that marvelous trick, it then makes morality radically relative to the wants and desires of a particular group or, of course, even each individual. Its conception of progress, of course, is the continuing expansion of economic demand and the industrial production to achieve it. This is what some call "growthism." If, as [the late theologian] Paul Tillich used to insist, religion means simply a group's "ultimate concern," then growthism would seem to be our religion and the gross national product our god. But all of that exacerbates the destructive and violent intrusion of human culture into nature.

It also leads to what [former Czech Republic President] Vaclav Havel has called "a demoralized culture" in which ethical ideals are simply reduced to the dreams of the consumer society or the lonely individuals who inhabit it. Finally, it brings about a culture of spiritual collapse in which there is no vision of a wider or deeper reality of which we are part than our own desires and dreams. That, of course, is precisely a spiritual emptiness or nihilism. Indeed, some commentators believe not only that this sense of spiritual emptiness is growing, but that it is leading to more profound social fragmentation and violence, including, quite evidently, the destruction of the family. As Richard Eckersley put it, our materialistically-oriented consumer society is increasingly failing

> to provide a sense of meaning, belonging, and purpose in our lives, as well as a framework of values. People need to have something to believe in and for, to feel they are part of a community and a valued member of society, and to have a sense of spiritual fulfillment—that is, a sense of relatedness and connectedness to the world and the universe in which they exist.[10]

David Bollier has argued in an issue of *Tikkun* [a Jewish journal of scholarship and reflection] that we must come to grips with this ethical and spiritual emptiness: "The truth is, Americans [today] need more than the First Amendment and its case law to bind them together. They need a new cultural covenant with each other that can begin frankly to address the spiritual void in modern secular society."[11]

At any rate, it is this materialist vision of prosperity, progress, and the good life that seems so rampant in our culture and so destructive to the environment. It is surely unworthy of free men and women. But that religiously oriented and practicing free men and women have shown little interest in questioning such a collapsed spiritual point-of-view from the perspective of their faith traditions— at least until recently—seems absolutely astounding! Can we seriously believe that God favors such materialism and growthism, especially insofar as they have brought about an unprecedented assault on creation itself? This is not an objection to freemarket economies. But to connect such market economies to the (albeit myopic) spiritual vision that the end and purpose of life (the good life) is a surfeit of material accumulation and security hardly seems worthy of such faiths. Are our religious traditions really so threadbare and lacking in imagination, so timid, that they reduce their visions of the life of faith to that of the consumer society?

On the one hand, some deconstructionists [philosophical investigators who have taken-apart current visions and understandings of the modern world] have argued that the lack (and from their point-of-view the impossibility) of any deeper or more encompassing vision of life is precisely a problem that cannot be overcome. It may be, on the other hand, that the very material culture that has led to such painful nihilism and that has brought such horrendous devastation upon the environment will, for those very reasons, inevitably lead us beyond its myopic perspective. "Despite claims by [social critics like] Lyotard and Frederick Jameson that our society reflects the absence of any great integrating vision or collective project, the great collective project has, in fact, presented itself. It is that of saving the earth—at this point, nothing else really matters."[12]

The need for a serious ethical response to nature and the environmental situation in which we find ourselves is, I believe, a third reason that the environment is a spiritual issue. If we are to change our abysmal behavior toward the environment, we will need more than scientific analysis and social legislation: We need a moral perspective and code that can help to change that behavior. As [U.S. Senator] Gaylord Nelson put it, "The harsh reality is that no war, no revolution, no peril in all of history measures up in importance to the threat of continued environmental deterioration. . . . The absence of a pervasive, guiding conservation ethic in our culture is the issue and the problem. It is a crippling if not, indeed, a fatal weakness.[13]

I find it interesting that until recently, "ethics" was a field in philosophy limited to human interaction. This was a reflection of our anthropocentric view that human beings lie outside or beyond nature. It is only humans who feel ethical obligation, and such obligation is directed only toward other human beings. In short, this view implied that we have no ethical obligations to individual plants and animals, never mind bioregions or nature as a whole because these entities have no "feelings" about how we treat them. I suppose this would be like a collection of trees agreeing—if they could—that unless you have roots, bark, and leaves you're beneath any sympathy or consideration. Fortunately, this myopic limitation of moral responsibility to human beings is now being seriously questioned.

Our system of dealing with nature simply as a collection of commodities put here for our privileged use seems to have failed or at least is in the process of failing. Aldo Leopold suggested that the only way to overcome our destructive treatment of nature is to treat it ethically, that is, as a *community* to which we belong. "All ethics so far evolved," he writes, "rest upon a single premise: That the individual is a member of a community of interdependent parts."[14] In other words, the new ecological ethic must extend our moral obligations to the larger community of nature to which we belong and that ultimately constitutes a single, interdependent web of entities) just as John Muir argued.

But how are we to jump from the biological "is" to the ethical "ought," from theory to actual behavior, from information to wisdom, from understanding to passionate caring? Science, especially the science of ecology, tells us that nature is a single community; how, then, do we *actually* come to love and respect it? The answer lies in going beyond its *utility for us* to a feeling-awareness of its *intrinsic value* in and of itself. As [the late Danish environmental philosopher] Arne Naess has put it, "The well-being and flourishing of human and nonhuman Life on Earth have value in themselves (synonyms: intrinsic value, inherent value). These values are independent of the usefulness of the nonhuman world for human purposes."[15]

But in order to do that, must we not, in fact, feel a reverence for this larger community to which we belong, must we not come to see it differently, in much the same way that Muir came to see it after the restoration of his sight, as God's holy creation? In other words, does not an effective ecological ethic, if it is to be more than an abstract set of principles, rest on a spiritual attitude toward the larger natural community to which we belong? Mustn't a serious and effective ecological ethics be grounded and founded upon a deeper and wider spiritual vision of life than seems available in the modern consumer societies (which interestingly enough have developed the very notion of utilitarian ethics)?

In a series of letters he wrote to his wife, Olga, while imprisoned [in 1982] by the Czechoslovakian Communist government, Vaclav Havel indicated that people living within modern industrial societies, whether capitalist or communist, all too often envisaged no wider, more encompassing, or more significant reality beyond their own needs and desires. Such a worldview, he thought, constitutes a kind of "demoralization."

> We live in an age in which there is a general turning away from Being: Our civilization, founded on a grand upsurge of science and technology, those great intellectual guides on how to conquer the world at the cost of losing touch with Being, transforms man its proud creator into a slave of his consumer needs. . . . A person who has been seduced by the consumer value system, whose identity is dissolved in an amalgam of the accoutrements of mass civilization, and who has no roots in the wider order of Being, no sense of responsi-

bility for any higher reality than his or her own personal survival, is a demoralized person and, by extension, a demoralized society.[16]

The result of this inability to envision ourselves as a part of a larger reality, whether divine or merely natural, has led, then, to a demoralized culture in which all too often we see ourselves as disembodied intellects who are "outside" or "above" nature and thus free to manipulate it for our own selfish ends. In short, it has led to a collapsed spiritual vision and moral stance in which, as we saw, nature is "beneath" us and not even thought to have "rights" or to call for moral obligations on our part. It is seen to be mere "stuff" put here for our enjoyment, simply the backdrop for the drama of the progressive unfolding of human history. [Former Vice President] Al Gore's book, *Earth in the Balance*, puts it this way: "Believing ourselves to be separate from the earth means having no idea how to fit into the natural cycle of life and no understanding of the natural processes of change that affect us and that we in turn are affecting. It means that we attempt to chart the course of civilization by reference to ourselves alone. No wonder we are lost and confused."[17]

This lack of awareness and appreciation for any "wider order of Being," as Havel put it, this "demoralization," has its roots, as we saw, in the spiritual worldview (how we "see" nature and life as a whole) that lies at the heart of our modern industrial cultures. Spiritual fire must be fought with spiritual fire. Any ethics on which we might pin our hopes of changing human behavior toward the environment must rest, ultimately, on a spiritual vision that transforms us, as it did Muir, and permits us to experience it in a reverential way as intrinsically valuable. If we are to change our behavior toward nature, if we are to act ethically toward it, we must look at it and our place within it differently. As Havel put it on another occasion, "The challenge offered by the post-Communist world is merely the current form of a broader and more profound challenge to discover a new type of self-understanding for man . . . we must discover a new relationship to our neighbors, and to the universe and its metaphysical order, which is the source of the moral order."[18]

In a Fourth of July speech in Philadelphia, Havel developed this theme further by grounding respect for others, including nature, in a more profound spiritual vision.

> Politicians at international forums may reiterate a thousand times that the basis of the new world order must be universal respect for human rights, but it will mean nothing as long as this imperative does not derive from the respect of the miracle of being, the miracle of the universe, the miracle of nature, the miracle of our own existence. Only someone who submits to the authority of the universal order . . . can genuinely value himself and his neighbors, and thus honor their rights as well.[19]

So this is another reason that the environment is a spiritual issue: Any ethical approach ultimately rests on a spiritual way of seeing it. It was Albert

Schweitzer [the famous Swiss doctor, theologian, musician, and missionary] who based his ethics on his spiritual sense of reverence for all life. He gained that reverence, he tells us in his autobiography, through an actual spiritual experience he had while crossing a river through a herd of hippopotami in Africa: "I am life which wills to live, in the midst of life which wills to live."[20] That experience of a reverence for life led Schweitzer to his explicit ethics, an ethics that parallels that of Aldo Leopold insofar as it links ethics and the wider natural community to which we belong.

> The great fault of all ethics heretofore has been that they believed themselves to have to deal only with the relations of man to man. In reality, however, the question is what is his attitude to the world and all life that comes within his reach. A man is ethical only when he devotes himself helpfully to all that is in need of help. Only the universal ethics of the feeling of responsibility in an ever-widening sphere for all that lives—only that ethic can be founded in thought. The ethic of the relation of man to man is not something apart by itself: It is only a particular relation which results from the universal one.[21]

Fourth and finally, there is a hunger across the land for a genuine spiritual vision and life beyond the constricted and narrowing confines of the consumer society. And where might we find such an encompassing sense of life as a meaningful whole if not within the universe or creation as a whole? That is, we are inextricably tied to both the earth community and the larger universe from which it has evolved. Can what Havel calls a wider vision of reality be other than Being or Reality itself, that is, the whole fecund fifteen-billion-year unfolding of the universe? There is a widespread thirst for "reality," especially on the part of our young. What could possibly be more real than reality itself, whether it be called nature, God, life, or the originating mystery that shines through that nature?

The fourth reason for thinking that the environment is a spiritual issue, then, lies in the fact that environmental concerns may make possible a genuine religious reform and renewal, not in the sense of dogma, but in the sense of experiencing with John Muir the epiphany that nature exhibits. It would seem that our time is calling us to awaken from our benumbed and bewitched state to a wonder at and reverence for the astonishing, miraculous, and mysterious creation of which we are a part. The whole world seems to arise in a mysterious emptiness. Reality is a transcendent but astonishing and holy power-to-be, an ever-flowing river of grace, a jaw-dropping gift of infinite giftedness. The gulf between nothing and something is filled with wonder, gratitude, and love of everything!

In a report to its General Assembly, the World Council of Churches expressed just this sense of the sacredness of nature in its own Christian imagery.

> Instead of a king relating to his realm, we picture God as the creator who "bodies forth" all that is, who creates not as a potter or an artist does, but more as a mother. That is to say, the universe, including our earth and its creatures and plants, "lives and moves and has its being" in God (cf. Acts 17:28), though

God is beyond and more than the universe. Organic images seem most appropriate for expressing both the immanence of God in and to the entire creation as well as God's transcendence of it. In the light of the incarnation, the whole universe appears to us as God's "body."[22]

The Unfurnished Eye

Yes, the environment is a spiritual issue. For that reason, religious consciousness and perspective are indispensable in ameliorating our present situation by helping us to integrate ourselves in a wider (and surely wiser) natural reality and by suggesting alternative conceptions of "progress" and the "good life:" "With current notions of economic growth at the root of so much of the earth's ecological deterioration, [what is called for is] a rethinking of our basic values and visions of progress."[23]

Unless and until we change our basic attitudes toward nature (and the relationship of God to nature) and our conceptions of what constitutes progress and the good life, further environmental devastation will be inevitable. What is called for, then, is a vision of how to live appropriately in the face of the truth of nature. We don't need to save the world; we need to love it. As Father Zosima puts it in Dostoevsky's *The Brothers Karamazov*, "Love all of God's creation, the whole and every grain of sand in it. Love every leaf, every ray of light. Love the animals, love the plants, love everything. If you love everything, you will perceive the divine mystery in things."[24]

And whether the extraordinary unfolding of life in its myriad forms is called God's creation, the Dao, the body of the Buddha, or just plain nature is not as important as perceiving it once again with a child's wild-eyed amazement. Rachel Carson certainly knew that.

> A child's world is fresh and new and beautiful, full of wonder and excitement. It is our misfortune that for most of us that clear-eyed vision, that true instinct for what is beautiful and awe-inspiring, is dimmed and even lost before we reach adulthood . . . I should ask that . . . each child in the world [develop] a sense of wonder so indestructible that it would last throughout life, as an unfailing antidote against the boredom and disenchantment of later years."[25]

In Emily Dickinson's marvelous phrase, to perceive it with "an unfurnished eye" is to see it as the epiphany it truly is; it is to see and feel the sanctity of life in all its wondrous forms. As was the case with John Muir, that just may be the way for us to find our ecological way home.

Notes

1 Linnie Marsh Wolfe, *Son of Wilderness: The Life of John Muir* (New York: Alfred Knopf, 1946), 104, 105.

2 William Frederic Bade, *The Life and Letters of John Muir* (Boston: Houghton Mifflin Co., 1924), 155.

3 John Wisdom, "Gods," in *Religion from Tolstoy to Camus*, ed. Walter Kaufmann (New York: Harper Torchbooks, 1964), 391-406.

4 For more on this view of religious understanding, see Paul Brockelman, *The Inside Story: A Narrative Approach to Religious Understanding and Truth* (Albany, NY: State University of New York Press, 1992).

5 Ralph Waldo Emerson, "Nature," in *The Portable Emerson*, ed. Carl Bode (New York: Penguin Books, 1981), 10.

6 *John of the Mountains: The Unpublished Journals of John Muir*, ed. Linnie Marsh Wolfe (Boston: Houghton Mifflin Co., 1938), 434.

7 In a very interesting article, Robert Kaplan argues that ecological disruptions will constitute the fundamental issue for our foreign relations in the years ahead. See Robert D. Kaplan, "The Coming Anarchy," *Atlantic Monthly,* February 1994, 44 ff.

8 Gordon Kaufmann, *In Face of Mystery: A Constructive Theology* (Cambridge, MA: Harvard University Press, 1993), 313.

9 Aldo Leopold, *A Sand County Almanac* (New York: Oxford University Press, 1949), viii.

10 Richard Eckersley, "The West's Deepening Cultural Crisis," *Futurist*, November/December 1993, 10.

11 David Bollier, "Who 'Owns' the Life of the Spirit?" *Tikkun*, January/February, 1994, 89.

12 Suzi Gablik, *The Reenchantment of Art* (New York: Thames and Hudson, 1991), 26.

13 Senator Gaylord Nelson, keynote speech, quoted in *EcoLetter*, North American Coalition on Religion and Ecology (NACRE), Washington, DC, 1993, 4.

14 Leopold, *A Sand County Almanac*, 203.

15 See Arne Naess, "The Deep Ecological Movement: Some Philosophical Aspects," *Philosophical Inquiry* 8, no. 1-2 (1981), 10-31.

16 Vaclav Havel, *Letters to Olga*, trans. Paul Wilson (New York: Knopf, 1988), 365-366.

17 Al Gore, *Earth in the Balance* (New York: Houghton Mifflin Co., 1992), 162-163.

18 Vaclav Havel, "The Post-Communist Nightmare," *New York Review of Books*, May 27, 1993, 10.

19 Vaclav Havel, "The New Measure of Man," *New York Times*, op-ed page, July 8, 1994.

20 Albert Schweitzer, *Out of My Life and Thought*, trans. C. T. Campion (New York: Henry Holt and Co., 1933), 186.

21 *Ibid.*, 188.

22 "Liberating Life: A Report to the World Council of Churches," in *Liberating Life: Contemporary Approaches to Ecological Theology*, ed. Charles Birch, William Eakin, and Jay B. McDaniel (Maryknoll, NY: Orbis Books, 1990), 279.

23 Sandra Postel, "Denial in the Decisive Decade," in *State of the World*, ed. Lester R. Brown (New York: W. W. Norton and Co., 1992), 4.

24 Fyodor M. Dostoevsky, *The Brothers Karamazov*, trans. R. Pevear and L. Volokhonskky (San Francisco: North Point Press, 1990), 119.

25 Rachel Carson, *The Sense of Wonder* (New York: Harper and Row, 1965), 42-43.

Introduction to article by Eric Katz

Faithful Jews strive to obey the 613 *mitzvot* (commandments) of the *Torah* (the "teaching" or "law" found in the Five Books of Moses—Genesis, Exodus, Leviticus, Numbers, and Deuteronomy). In this article, Eric Katz stresses that Jewish teachings on the environment are grounded in specific commandments binding on all Jews, for nature is a realm in which humans interact with God.

Based on the foundational, theocentric understanding that the earth belongs to God—and is not a human possession—Katz argues that although humans have the power to use natural resources, and necessarily do so, this human role has limitations, not "unrestricted license." In this regard, he highlights several limiting principles such as *yishuv ha-aretz* (restricting what animals may be raised and which plants may be used), *tza'ar ba'alei chayim* (compassion for animals), and *bal tashchit* (prohibition against wanton destruction).

Nature as Subject:
Human Obligation and Natural Community

Eric Katz

Judaism and the Ecological Crisis

What does Judaism say about nature and the environmental crisis? Any discussion of the Jewish view of the natural world, the ecological principles underlying natural processes, and the obligations relevant to human activity in relation to nature must begin with the concrete and specific commandments binding upon all practicing Jews. A so-called worldview of Judaism would be a mere abstraction from the specific rules and principles of Jewish life, for in Judaism, perhaps more than any other religion, philosophical meaning arises out of the procedure of concrete daily activity. As Robert Gordis writes: "The true genius of Judaism has always lain in specifics." Thus, Gordis continues, an understanding of Jewish teachings on the environmental crisis is "not to be sought in high-sounding phrases which obligate [Jews] to nothing concrete; rather [it] will be found in specific areas of Jewish law and practice."[1]

This reluctance to focus on abstract philosophical principles or a generalized worldview as a replacement for concrete obligations regarding the natural environment is a recurrent theme in the expositions of contemporary commentators on the Jewish tradition. After a discussion of the Hebrew concepts of nature in the Bible, Jeanne Kay concludes, in part, that "the Bible views observance of its commandments, rather than specific attitudes toward nature or techniques of resource protection, as the prerequisite of a sound environment."[2] In an essay, E. L. Allen claims that in the Jewish tradition nature is neither an abstraction nor an ideal, but rather one of the realms in which humans interact with God. "Nature is envisaged as one of the spheres in which God meets man personally and in which he is called upon to exercise responsibility."[3] Thus, "for the man of the Bible, nature is never seen in abstraction either from God or from the tasks which He has assigned to man in the world."[4] Within Judaism, then, the human view of nature and the environment is grounded in the specific obligations and activities of Jewish life, the tasks and commandments that God presented to the Jewish people.

Subdue the Earth: Dominion and Stewardship

Given this turn away from the abstract, an examination of the Jewish perspective on nature and the environmental crisis must begin with specific texts and commands, and none is more important than Genesis 1:28 in which God commands humanity to subdue the earth:

> And God blessed them [Adam and Eve]; and God said unto them: "Be fruitful and multiply, and replenish the earth, and subdue it; and have dominion over the fish of the sea, and over the fowl of the air, and over every living thing that moves upon the earth."

This notorious passage appears in almost every discussion of the religious foundations of the environmental crisis. It is used by Lynn White, Jr., and others, to demonstrate that the Judeo-Christian tradition is fundamentally biased toward the dominion—if not the actual domination—of the earth by humanity.[5] It suggests that the earth and all nonhuman living beings in nature belong to the human race, mere means for the growth ("be fruitful and multiply") of humanity.

This is not the place for a full discussion of White's controversial thesis concerning the tradition.[6] But if we are to understand the Jewish perspective on the environmental crisis, we must examine the meaning of the command to "subdue" the earth and its relationship to the process of domination. Does this passage represent God's gift of title to humanity? Does this passage mean that the earth belongs to the human race?

The Jewish tradition clearly answers in the negative. Norman Lamm points out that the very next line from Genesis, which is usually ignored in the discussions of this passage, restricts humans to a vegetarian diet, hardly the prerogative of one who has dominion, control, and ownership of all the living creatures in nature! "And God said: 'Behold, I have given you every herb yielding seed, which is upon the earth, and every tree in which is the fruit of a tree yielding seed—to you shall it be for food'" (Genesis 1:29). The Torah [the Books of Moses, the first five books of the Hebrew Bible—Genesis, Exodus, Leviticus, Numbers, and Deuteronomy] thus limits the human right to "subdue" and use nature; this command is not title to unbridled domination.[7]

Indeed, Jewish scholars throughout history have gone to extraordinary lengths to disavow any idea that Genesis 1:28 permits the subjugation of nature by humanity. The Talmud (*Yebemot* 65b) [commentary by rabbis on the Torah] relates the phrase "subdue it" to the first part of the sentence, "be fruitful and multiply," and then through a tortuous piece of logic, connecting the act of "subduing" with warfare—a male activity—claims that the passage really means that the propagation of the human race is an obligation of the male. And the medieval commentators Nachmanides and Obadiah Sforno connect the phrase to the activities of humanity in the use of natural resources, not their destruction or misuse. Nachmanides sees the passage as granting permission to humanity to continue their activities of building, agriculture, and mining. Sforno's explanation is even more restrictive: "*And subdue it*—that you protect yourself with your reason and prevent the animals from entering within your boundaries and you rule over them."[8] These interpretations recognize the power of humanity to use natural resources, and indeed the necessity of them so doing, but they emphasize limitations in the human role. Dominion here does not mean unrestricted domination.

The reason for the restriction is also clear: In the Jewish tradition, humanity is the steward of the natural world, not its owner. Stewardship is a position that acknowledges the importance of the human role in the care and maintenance of the natural world without permitting an unrestricted license. David Ehrenfeld and Philip Bentley thus consider it a middle position, but one that is definitely on the side of the spectrum that advocates the human use of the natural environment, rather than the opposite extreme of the sacred reverence and noninterference with nature suggested by Eastern religions.[9] To use a comparison widespread in the literature of environmental philosophy, the concept of stewardship in Judaism advocates neither the *domination-destruction* nor the *preservation* of the natural environment but its *conservation* and wise developmental use. Genesis 2:15 lends support to the idea of stewardship, as it declares: "And . . . God . . . put him into the garden of Eden to till it and to keep it." This suggests, as Ehrenfeld and Bentley point out, that the human domination over nature should not be interpreted in a harsh or exploitative way, and the rabbinic tradition has not done so.[10] The whole idea of stewardship implies care for an entity that is in one's power; it does not imply exploitative use.

The idea of care implicit in stewardship is, however, based on a more fundamental concept: The proper ownership of the entity under care. From a mere analysis of the meaning of concepts, the difference between dominion and stewardship is that the former includes an unrestricted ownership and total power over the subordinate entity, while the latter strictly limits power because it denies ownership. Humanity does not own the natural world. *In Judaism, the world belongs to God.* Judaism is a theocentric religion at least when it concerns the relationships between humans and nature. God himself, not human life and welfare, is the source of all religious and moral obligation. The divine ownership of nature is most clearly and directly stated in Psalm 24: "The earth is the Lord's and the fulness thereof, the world and those who dwell therein." Humanity cannot have an unrestricted dominion over the natural world because the world belongs to God; humanity is merely the divinely-appointed guardian or steward of what belongs to God.

This general theocentric worldview is expressed in many ways throughout Jewish ritual and practice, so much so that Jonathan Helfand can declare that "in both content and spirit, the Jewish tradition negates the arrogant proposal that the earth is man's unqualified dominion."[11] God does not forsake the ownership of the world when he instructs Adam and his descendants to master it. As Helfand notes, the existence of the laws concerning the sabbatical—and the Jubilee—year clearly indicate that God is the owner of the earth: "And the land is not to be sold in perpetuity, for all land is Mine, because you are strangers and sojourners before Me" (Leviticus 25:23).[12] In Samuel Belkin's words, man possesses but a "temporary tenancy of God's creation."[13] Thus, the prohibition on farming the land in the seventh years, which is detailed in Leviticus 25:3-4, is not to be understood as a primitive attempt at enlightened agricultural methods. Belkin argues that "the sages refuse to assign purely economic, agricultural, or social motives to this law," for Rabbi Abahu cites the ownership of God as the primary reason for the existence of the Sabbath and Jubilee years (*Sanhedrin* 39a).[14] Belkin himself is even more emphatic about the theocentrism of Judaism: "The entire structure of Judaism rests" on the principle "that creation belongs to the Creator." Without such a principle, humans would own the world and the entities within it; they would then be able to use those things without regard to any law or principles other than their own will. But this is not the case: The moral code of the Torah, the ritual commands, and the laws of Judaism all strongly imply that the world belongs to God, and God has "instructed man concerning what he is permitted to do or prohibited from doing with His creation . . . [God] alone dictates the terms of man's tenancy in this world."[15]

One commonplace example of the way ritual action reinforces the notion of God's ownership is the commandment concerning the blessings over food. Helfand cites the *Tosefta: Berakhot* 4:1:

> Man may not taste anything until he has recited a blessing, as it is written: "The earth is the Lord's and the fullness thereof." Anyone who derives benefit from this world without a [prior] blessing is guilty of misappropriating sacred property.[16]

The fact that God owns the world requires us to ask permission before we ingest any item of food. All the objects of the material world are as sacred as the entities of heaven, for they are all the creation of God, and belong to God.[17]

Perhaps the significance of the theocentric ownership of the world by God in Judaism is best summarized by the rituals concerning not the sabbatical year, but the ordinary *weekly* Sabbath. Ehrenfeld and Bentley articulate the meaning of the Sabbath for contemporary environmentalists: "For Jews, it is the Sabbath and the idea of the Sabbath that introduces the necessary restraint into stewardship."[18] For these authors, the Sabbath acquires this meaning because of three elements of the observance of Sabbath: "We create nothing, we destroy nothing, and we enjoy the bounty of the Earth." The fact that nothing is created serves to remind us that we are not as supreme as God; the fact that nothing is destroyed emphasizes that the world does not belong to us, but to God; and our enjoyment of the earth's bounty reminds us that God is the source of nature's goodness.[19] Thus, the concept of the Sabbath itself—(the absence of work and the appreciation of God—imposes a strict limit on human activity and achievement.) Humanity in no way possesses dominion over the nonhuman world since it does not even possess dominion over its own activities.

Observance of the Sabbath thus returns us to the notion of stewardship, for without dominion, humanity is merely the steward of God's creation. But stewardship strongly implies a notion of responsibility, for the steward is responsible for the condition for the entities in his care. To illustrate this point, Ehrenfeld and Bentley recount a story told by the eleventh-century Spanish rabbi, Jonah ibn Janah: A man walks into a house in the midst of a deserted city; he finds a table with good food and drink and begins to eat, thinking to himself, "I deserve all this, it is mine, I will act as I please." Little does he know that the owners are watching him, and that he will have to pay for all that he consumes. Thus, man, as merely the appointed steward of God's creation, is responsible to God for the use of God's property, the natural world.[20]

Environmentalism in Practice Rituals and Commandments

An abstract notion of responsibility for the guardianship of the natural world is not, however, an adequate account of Judaism's perspective on the environmental crisis. For this notion of responsibility to be part of the practice of religious belief, it must be distilled into a series of specific commandments regarding human actions affecting the natural world. An examination of Jewish law and ritual does reveal these specific commandments, involving many different aspects of everyday Jewish life.

Several commandments involve the general health and well-being of the human community as it is situated in the natural environment. Deuteronomy 23:13-15, for example, requires the burial of human sewage in wartime, with the command that the soldiers must possess a spade for that very purpose among their other weapons: "And it shalt be when thou sittest down outside, thou shalt dig therewith, and shalt turn back and cover that which cometh from thee."[21] A more general principle is *yishuv ha-aretz* ("the settling of the land") which mandates both restrictions on the type of animals that can be raised and the type of trees that could be used for burning on the sacrificial altar. Goats and sheep were thought to be destructive to the land, and vine and olive trees were too valuable to be used in religious services.[22] Helfand argues that *yishuv ha-aretz* is also the basis of the mandate to establish a *migrash*, an open space one thousand cubits wide around all cities in Israel, in which agriculture and building would be prohibited. "The operative principle . . . calls upon the Jew in his homeland to balance the economic, environmental, and even religious needs of society carefully to assure the proper development and setting of the land."[23]

The existence of the *migrash* is, indeed, only one aspect of the laws regulating life in early Jewish cities, what amounts to a fully realized notion of town planning. Aryeh Carmell discusses many of these restrictions in an essay detailing the rabbinic concern for the quality of the environment in Jewish life.[24]

Rambam in the *Hilchot Shechenim* ("Laws of Neighborly Relations") explains that there are four classes of nuisance in which injury is always presumed: Smoke, dust, noxious smells, and vibration. There is also a right to quietness.[25] This leads to rabbinic regulations—a kind of ancient zoning ordinance—regarding the specific placement of certain "industries" within the town: Threshing floors, cemeteries, tanneries, and slaughterhouses.[26] The basis of these rabbinic regulations was a limitation of individual property rights for the sake of the entire community.[27] It seems clear that these limitations of individual property rights can also be traced to the notion that all property belongs ultimately to God, and thus that the use of the property by human individuals must be regulated by the laws of the Torah and the rabbinical interpretations of these laws.

Another category of Jewish law concerns the human relation to the divine plan. Nature is conceived, in Judaism, as the result of a divine plan or intelligence, which is not to be altered by human activity. Thus, in Leviticus 19:19, we find a prohibition against the hybridization of plants and animals, and even a restriction on wearing two types of cloth: "You shall not let your cattle mate with a different kind, you shall not sow your field with two kinds of seed, you shall not wear a garment of wool and linen." Helfand explains that this passage falls in the midst of a discussion of the proper and improper forms of human relationships, thereby reinforcing the idea that there is a fixed divine plan for both the social and the natural order of the universe.[28] The intrinsic significance of the divine plan is further revealed by Jewish traditions that aim, in modern terminology, to protect endangered species. Thus, Helfand cites the commentator Nachmanides on the meaning of two biblical commands—not to slaughter a cow and her calf on the same day (Leviticus 22:28) and not to take a mother bird with her young (Deuteronomy 22:6): "Scripture will not permit a destructive act that will cause the extinction of a species."[29]

A concern for animals is further emphasized in Jewish thought by the fundamental principle of *tza'ar ba'alei chayim* ("the pain of living creatures"). Although it is not strictly a principle concerning the ethical treatment of the environment, it is the basis for the compassionate treatment of animals through Jewish life. Gordis considers it one of the two basic principles constituting the Jewish attitude to the nonhuman natural world—the second principle, *bal tashchit*, will be discussed below.[30] *Tza'ar ba'alei chayim* requires a concern for the well-being of all living beings—if not a full-scale sacred reverence for all life, at least an attitude of universal compassion.[31] The laws of kosher slaughtering, as well as the law forbidding the yoking together of animals of unequal strength (Deuteronomy 22:10), are based on this compassion for animal suffering.

As Gordis emphasizes, one of the most unlikely textual affirmations for *tza'ar ba'alei chayim* is the conclusion of the book of Jonah, in which Jonah complains to God about the destruction of a gourd, a plant that had been shielding Jonah from the sun as he awaited God's decision about the destruction of the city of Nineveh. Job is angry for two reasons: God has spared the city, thereby making Jonah's prophecy appear foolish or pointless; and God has caused the gourd that shaded him to wither and die. God's reply is this:

> You pity the gourd, for which you did not labor, nor did you make it grow,
> which came into being in a night, and perished in a night. And should I not pity
> Nineveh, that great city, in which there are more than a hundred and twenty
> thousand persons who do not know their right hand from their left, and also
> much cattle? (Jonah 4:9-11)

God's rebuke compels a consideration of three different kinds of entities—
the human inhabitants of Nineveh, the nonhuman domesticated animals that live
in Nineveh, and the wild gourd—the plant life—outside the city. Clearly God
does not consider the potential loss of the cattle to be a minor point; the loss of
the cattle with the human population is an event to pity, an event requiring divine compassion. But the passage also suggests that pity for the gourd—wild,
undomesticated plant life—is not an absurdity. Jonah's mistake is not that he felt
compassion for the gourd, but that his level of concern was too great. It is wrong
to value the wild gourd more than God values the inhabitants of Nineveh. Compassion for all living beings is a moral obligation in Judaism, but the context
will determine the appropriate level of response.

Bal Tashchit: Do Not Destroy

Although the preceding section listed several principle and commandments
that prescribe specific actions regarding the nonhuman environment, the most
important and fundamental principle of the Jewish response to nature is *bal
tashchit*—"do not destroy"—which is first outlined in Deuteronomy 20:19-20:

> When you besiege a city for a long time . . . you shall not destroy its trees
> by wielding an ax against them. You may eat of them, but you may not cut
> them down. Are the trees in the field men that they should be besieged by you?
> Only the trees which you know are not trees for food, you may destroy and cut
> down, that you may build siege-works against the city.

In the context of warfare, specific moral rules apply. As Gordis notes, "This
injunction ran counter to accepted procedures in ancient war," particularly the
actions of the ruthless Assyrians.[32] But more importantly, the principle of *bal
tashchit* forbids the wanton destruction of an enemy's resources, a so-called
scorched-earth policy of warfare. Lamm comments that "what the Torah pro-
scribed is not the use of the trees to win a battle, which may often be a matter of
life and death, but the wanton destruction of embattled areas, so as to render
them useless to the enemy should he win."[33]

The principle here is the prohibition on wanton destruction or vandalism,
the destruction of trees for no (or little) redeeming purpose. Lamm also notes
that Jewish law extends the law to situations in peacetime as well as war; the
Bible merely used an example of a situation in wartime to emphasize the seriousness of the restriction, for the commandment "do not destroy" is so powerful

that it cannot even be overridden for the sake of victory in war.[34] Thus, both Lamm and Gordis claim that *bal tashchit* is the establishment of a general principle in the expression of a concrete situation.[35]

There is much evidence from rabbinical texts to support the idea that *bal tashchit* is a general and fundamental principle regarding human actions with the nonhuman and natural environment. The idea of "wielding an ax" is extended to any means of destruction, even the diverting of a water supply.[36] Moreover, the principle is extended to any natural entity or to any human artifact. In the *Sefer Hahinuch* ("Shoftim" Commandment 529) is written this comment on *bal tashchit*: "In addition [to the cutting down of trees], we include the negative commandment that we should not destroy anything, such as burning or tearing clothes, or breaking a utensil—without purpose." Lamm also cites Maimonides, who includes the stopping of fountains, the wasting of food, or "wrecking that which is built" as violations of *bal tashchit*.[37] Thus, Gordis concludes: "The principle of *bal tashchit* entered deep into Jewish consciousness, so that the aversion to vandalism became an almost psychological reflex, and wanton destruction was viewed with loathing and horror by Jews for centuries."[38]

The precise meaning of *bal tashchit* and its application in the affairs of humans interacting with and using natural objects raises, however, interesting issues. First is the relationship of *bal tashchit* to economic considerations. The original passage in Deuteronomy appears to make a distinction between food-producing (fruit-bearing) trees and trees that do not produce fruit. Although wanton destruction is prohibited regarding all trees, fruit-bearing trees should be protected even from appropriate military uses. It is permitted to destroy trees that do not produce fruit for good reasons. Lamm explains that this special concern for food-producing trees may be tied to commercial considerations, either "an economy of scarcity" or the existence of property rights. And there is rabbinical evidence for the importance of economic values: A fruit-bearing tree may be destroyed if the land is needed for the construction of a house. These exceptions to *bal tashchit* are not permitted for purely aesthetic reasons, such as landscaping.[39] Eric Freudenstein echoes this conclusion (which he derives from *Baba Kama* 91b): "The standards of *bal tashchit* are relative, not absolute. The law is interpreted in the Talmud [rabbinic commentary on Torah, Jewish law] as limited to purposeless destruction and does not prohibit destruction for the sake of economic gain."[40] But Freudenstein supplements this conclusion with the point that what constitutes an appropriate economic value differs from generation to generation, and thus the correct use of *bal tashchit* at any time must be left to the authorities to decide. The keeping of goats and sheep was once banned because of the destructive impact on the environment, but it is now permitted.[41] Thus, the moral evaluation for the destruction of an object or natural entity will depend on the economic and social context of the act. *Bal tashchit* prohibits *wanton* destruction, but the meaning of "wanton" will change throughout history.

An additional economic issue is the relationship of *bal tashchit* to the notions of private property. Both Lamm and Gordis claim that the principle is not tied in any way to our modern notion of private property; one is not permitted to destroy one's own property any more than one is permitted to destroy another's. *Bal tashchit* is concerned with "the waste of an economic value *per se*," i.e., the social utility of the object being destroyed. Lamm even cites the interpretation of the principle to include the idea that it is permissible to destroy a fruit tree if it is somehow damaging the property of others—thus, the basis of the principle would be social concern. *Bal tashchit* is a religious and moral law that requires a consideration of the social implications of actions that harm nonhuman entities; it is not a law of financial and personal property.[42]

But even this focus on social consequences does not reveal the true depth of *bal tashchit*. Questions of private property and social utility reintroduce the issue of the real ownership of the world. It was noted above that the fundamental basis of the idea of stewardship was the theocentric perspective of Judaism: The world belongs to God. When *bal tashchit* is combined with this theocentrism, we arrive at the ultimate argument against the destruction of natural entities: Such entities are the property of God. This position easily renders insignificant the economic or utilitarian justifications for *bal tashchit*. The principle is not designed to make life better for humanity; it is not meant to insure a healthy and productive environment for human beings. In the terminology of environmental philosophy, it is not an *anthropocentric* [human-centered] principle at all: Its purpose is not to guarantee or promote human interests. The purpose of *bal tashchit* is to maintain respect for God's creation.

Gordis thus ties *bal tashchit* to the laws of the sabbatical year and the Jubilee year—the reaffirmation of God's ownership of the land.[43] But as an explanation of the philosophical worldview that underlies *bal tashchit*, I find sections of the book of Job even more compelling. Near the end of the story, Job is finally able to question God about the reasons for the several misfortunes that have befallen him. God speaks to Job out of the whirlwind, but God's answer is not a direct justification of the seemingly incomprehensible divine actions that have radically altered Job's life. Instead, God discusses aspects of the natural world—the wild domain outside of human control—and challenges Job to acknowledge the limits of human wisdom:

> Where was thou when I laid the foundations of the earth?
> Declare, if thou hast the understanding.
> Who determined the measures thereof, if thou knowest?
> Or who stretched the line upon it?

(Job 38:4-5)

And God continues to paint a picture of a world that exists independent of human concerns and free from human notions of rationality or cause and effect:

> Who hath cleft a channel for the waterflood,
> Or a way for the lightning of the thunder;

On the wilderness, wherein there is no man;
To satisfy the desolate and waste ground,
And to cause the bud of the tender herb to spring forth?

(Job 38:25-27)

And more than the useless rain on land where humans do not live, there are the animals, the great beasts "behemoth" and "leviathan," which do not exist for human purposes; they lie outside the sphere of human life (Job 40:15ff).

God's speech to Job out of the whirlwind is a dramatic reaffirmation of the theocentrism of the universe, God's creation. Job, as well as any other human being, errs when he believes that the events of the world must have a rational explanation relevant to human life. The events of the world are ultimately explained only in reference to God. This theocentrism is the driving force of *bal tashchit*, for it gives meaning to the reasons behind a prohibition on wanton destruction. Destruction is not an evil because it harms human life—we humans should not believe that God sends the rain for us—it is an evil because it harms the realm of God and God's creation.

The remarkable philosophical conclusion from this perspective of theocentrism is that it serves to resolve a long-standing dispute among secular environmental philosophers: Should anthropocentric (i.e., human-centered) or nonanthropocentric arguments be used to support environmental practices? Should policies of environmental preservation be pursued because such policies will benefit humanity, or because such policies are *intrinsically* beneficial to the natural world? Both positions encounter ethical and policy-oriented problems. The anthropocentric perspective would permit the use (and destruction) of natural entities for a corresponding greater human benefit; but the nonanthropocentric intrinsic value perspective implies a policy of strict nonintervention in natural processes, an absolute sanctity of nature. One position may lead to the destruction of nature, and the other may lead to worshipful noninterference: Thus, the dilemma for environmental philosophers.

On a practical level, the theocentrism of Judaism resolves this dilemma because it is functionally equivalent to a nonanthropocentric doctrine of the intrinsic value of nature without endorsing the sacredness of natural entities in themselves. Natural objects are valued, and cannot be destroyed, because they belong to God. They are sacred, not in themselves, but because of God's creative process. This worldview is, in part, derived from the Kabbalistic [mystical] strand of Jewish thought, as is expressed quite clearly by David Shapiro: "The quality of loving kindness is the basis of all creation. It is God's steadfast love that brought this world into being, and it is His steadfast love that maintains it."[44] Thus, "all creation is linked together in a bond of unity," which humans must act to preserve and not to destroy.[45] A further description of this view is offered by Lamm, who writes that "Judaism . . . refuses to ascribe the quality of holiness to nature and natural objects as such."[46] The Jewish view of the human relationship to nature can be represented by the opposition of two extreme views, with the mainstream Jewish tradition taking the middle position. On the one side is the form of Hasidism [extremely conservative Judaism, concerned with preserving and upholding traditional Jewish thought, practice, and ritual] that follows the Kabbalistic tradition of God's immanence throughout nature, the extreme of nature-deification. On the other side is the Mitnagdic criticism of Hasidism which radically separates the divine and natural realms, the extreme of nature-as-profane. Lamm argues that the two extremes tend to converge, for the Hasidic tradition teaches respect for nature without ascribing sanctity to it, while the Mitnagdic tradition acknowledges that from God's perspective the world is suffused with God's presence. For Lamm, this "theological tension is resolve . . . [in] . . . practice . . . [as] Nature is not to be considered holy, but neither is one permitted to act ruthlessly towards it, needlessly to ravage it and disturb its integrity."[47] As Gordis concludes, "every natural object is an embodiment of the creative power of God and is therefore sacred."[48] Its sacredness and its integrity—its intrinsic value, let us say—rests on its status as God's creation. Thus, it is the theocentric basis of *bal tashchit* that requires Jews to act with a practical respect for the value of nature without regard to human concerns.

The Jewish View of Nature

This survey of Jewish principles and commandments regarding nature and the environment does not lead easily into a unified worldview. Is it possible to summarize this examination of the specific regulations of Judaism concerning nature? Is there a coherent Jewish perspective? Yes: The Jewish worldview holds that nature has a value independent of human interests, as an expression of the creative power of God. This divinely-inspired value thus inspires respect and requires obedience on the part of humanity, the servants and stewards of God's creation.

As stewards of God's earth, humans serve as partners in the never-ending task of perfecting the universe. Gordis concludes that "Judaism . . . insists that human beings have an obligation not only to conserve the world of nature, but to enhance it" as a "co-partner with God in the work of creation."[49] The universe is God's creation, and that is the undeniable and fundamental starting point of the Jewish view of nature. Understanding the universe as an outgrowth of God's power is the most important aspect of the value of nature in the Jewish worldview. It gives the natural world a force, a presence, that cannot be ignored.

Allen ends his discussion of the value of nature with a return to the Book of Job, for in God's speech out of the whirlwind we are presented with the essence of the wild: A world beyond the control and understanding of humanity. But the lack of control does not breed disrespect; on the contrary, it creates a sense of awe, wonder, and responsibility, for we are in the presence of the divine. "The untamed world beyond the frontiers of human society is fraught with the numinous, it is a constant reminder that man is not master in the world, but only a privileged and therefore responsible inhabitant of it."[50]

Notes

1 Robert Gordis, "Judaism and the Environment," *Congress Monthly* 57, No. 6 (September/October 1990), 8.

2 Jeanne Kay, "Concepts of Nature in the Hebrew Bible," *Environmental Ethics* 10 (1988), 326-327.

3 E. L. Allen, "The Hebrew View of Nature," *The Journal of Jewish Studies* 2, No. 2 (1951), 100.

4 *Ibid.*

5 Lynn White, Jr., "The Historical Roots of Our Ecologic Crisis," *Science* 155 (1967), 1203-1207.

6 For a more philosophical discussion, see John Passmore, *Man's Responsibility for Nature: Ecological Problems and Western Traditions* (New York: Scribner's, 1974), 3-40, and Robin Attfield, *The Ethics of Environmental Concern* (New York: Columbia University Press, 1983), 20-87.

7 Norman Lamm, "Ecology and Jewish Law and Theology," in *Faith and Doubt* (New York: KTAV, 1971), 164-165.,

8 Gordis, *op. cit.,* 7-8.

9 David Ehrenfeld and Philip J. Bentley, "Judaism and the Practice of Stewardship," *Judaism* 34 (1985), 301-302.

10 *Ibid.,* 305.

11 Jonathan I. Helfand, "The Earth Is the Lord's: Judaism and Environmental Ethics," in *Religion and the Environmental Crisis*, ed. Eugene C. Hargrove (Athens: University of Georgia Press, 1986), 39.

12 *Ibid.,* 40.

13 Samuel Belkin, "Man as Temporary Tenant," in *Judaism and Human Rights,* ed. Milton R. Konvitz (New York: Norton, 1972), 253.

14 *Ibid.,* 253-254.

15 *Ibid.,* 255.

16 Helfand, *op. cit.,* 40-41.

17 Belkin, *op. cit.,* 252.

18 Ehrenfeld and Bentley, *op. cit.,* 309.

19 *Ibid.,* 310.

20 *Ibid.,* 306-307.

21 See discussion in Eric G. Freudenstein, "Ecology and the Jewish Tradition," *Judaism* 19 (1970), 409-410.

22 Helfand, *op. cit.,* 46.

23 *Ibid.*

24 Aryeh Carmell and Cyril Domb, ed., "Judaism and the Quality of the Environment," in *Challenge: Torah Views on Science and Its Problems* (New York: Feldheim, 1978), 500-525.

25 *Ibid.,* 503.

26 *Ibid.,* 504.

27 *Ibid.,* 505.

28 Helfand, *op. cit.,* 42.

29 *Ibid.,* 45.

30 Gordis, *op. cit.,* 8.

31 Allen, *op. cit.,* 103.

32 Gordis, *op. cit.,* 9.

33 Lamm, *op. cit.,* 169.

34 *Ibid.*
35 Lamm, *loc. cit.*
36 Gordis, *loc. cit.*
37 Lamm, *loc. cit.*
38 Gordis, *loc. cit.*
39 Lamm, *op. cit.,* 170.
40 Freudenstein, *op. cit.,* 411.
41 *Ibid.,* 411-412.
42 Lamm, *op. cit.,* 171-172.
43 Gordis, *loc.cit.*
44 David S. Shapiro, "God, Man, and Creation," *Tradition* 15 (1975), 25.
45 *Ibid.,* 41.
46 Lamm, *op. cit.,* 173.
47 *Ibid.,* 173-177.
48 Gordis, *op. cit.,* 10.
49 *Ibid.,* citing *B. Shabbat* 10a.
50 Allen, *op. cit.,* 103.

Introduction to article by Iain Provan

In the Hebrew Bible/Christian Old Testament, it is clear from the opening chapters of Genesis that God is the Creator of the *cosmos* and as such, it is God's; thus, all creatures—including human creatures—belong to God. As a result, and in this article, Iain Provan asserts that human beings, though they name the other creatures, do not have authority over them; that human beings, though they bear the image of God, are not transcendent over nature; and that human beings, though they rule the rest of creation, do not do so solely for human benefit. Humans are dually *earth-keepers* and *people-keepers.*

The Land Is Mine and You Are Only Tenants:
Earth-keeping and People-keeping in the Old Testament

Iain Provan

What kind of story is the biblical story? Does it help us with earth-keeping and people-keeping, or hinder us in these endeavors? It is commonly alleged nowadays that it *hinders*—that people who have taken the Bible story as their governing story have a woeful record of looking after the earth and have often not treated human beings very well either. This is not the place to explore the full truthfulness of such claims about what Christians have sometimes done or not done, historically. There is certainly some truth to be found in such critiques, but there is also much ignorance and propaganda. More to the point is whether the biblical narrative itself has *required* such Christians to act negligently or badly, where they *have* so acted, or whether the biblical narrative itself presents a quite different vision of the world from the one pursued by these badly-behaved Christians, perhaps sometimes misunderstood and misconstrued by its readers. I would certainly want to argue the latter: That the problem lies—where there has been a problem—not with the Bible, but only with certain very inadequate readings of the Bible. In fact, the biblical story in itself provides us with important resources—Christians would say, *ultimately* important resources, provided by God himself—in our quest to be both earth-keepers and people-keepers, and indeed to understand the interrelationship between these two. I want to show some ways in which this is so, focusing on the Old Testament Scriptures, and within these Scriptures on the early chapters [of the Book] of Genesis. This is not only because of the importance of the early chapters of Genesis to a Christian worldview, but also because of the practical matter of the length available for this presentation. Towards the end, I shall nevertheless begin to branch out to some extent into the remainder of the Old Testament, so that we get a fuller picture of biblical teaching. My tendency, incidentally, will be to say more about earth-keeping than people-keeping. This is not because I think that the first is more important than the second, but only because I think Christians have more often understood the imperatives surrounding the second than those surrounding the first.

The Cosmos Has a Creator

Fundamental to the biblical vision of the world are the opening chapters of Genesis. It is here that we first learn to call the thing that we are involved in day-by-day "Creation" rather than "Nature." *In the beginning God created*, proclaims Genesis 1—a God who is personal and moral, and has tremendous interest in what God has created and what is for its good. Before God creates, there is only *tohu wabohu* (Genesis 1:2), a Hebrew phrase referring to the formlessness and emptiness of the cosmos. In God's creating, God *both* provides the "form," giving the cosmos a particular structure and shape, *and* makes an empty place full—full of life. This terra-forming, first, finds light separated from darkness, the heavens from the earth, the earth from the seas, and the earth is given a particular character as a plant-producing place. The earth is made habitable. This shaped but empty place is then, secondly, provided with inhabitants for each of its spheres—luminaries for the heavens, birds and sea creatures for air and the seas, and land creatures for the earth. In this "speaking" of creation into being, the distribution of God's words perhaps already indicates a certain hierarchy of importance in creation, or at least a certain focus of interest—there is much more to be said on the sixth day (over 80 Hebrew words) than on the first (2 Hebrew words). The spotlight in Genesis 1 falls upon the earth rather than upon the heavens; and on the earth, it falls upon the land creatures above all other creatures. Among the land creatures, it falls upon the human creatures especially—those who are said to have been made in God's own image and likeness. What Genesis 1 suggests by identifying the fashioning of human creatures in this way as a *crucial moment* of God's creation, Genesis 2 also suggests by making human beings the *center* of God's creation, in which plants and herbs cannot appear before there are people to work the ground (Genesis 2:5), and indeed we do not hear of trees, animals and birds until after human creation has been accomplished (2:9, 19-20). The interest of both passages has little to do with chronology, but everything to do with different strategies for emphasizing the importance of human beings in the context of creation.

Is Biblical Creation Theology Destructively Anthropocentric?

It is this conviction about the importance of human beings in creation that has brought the Bible into disrepute in some quarters in recent times, as the impact of such beings on the remainder of creation has become an important matter of debate. Many will know of the famous essay from 1967 by Lynn White, Jr., "The Historical Roots of Our Ecologic Crisis." Claiming to describe what it is that Christianity has told people historically about their relations with their environment, he writes as follows:

Lynh White

> By gradual stages a loving and all-powerful God had created light and darkness, the heavenly bodies, the earth and its plants, animals, birds and fishes. Finally, God had created Adam and, as an afterthought, Eve, to keep man from being lonely. Man named all the animals, thus establishing his dominance over them. God planned all of this explicitly for man's benefit and rule: No item in the physical creation had any purpose save to serve man's purposes. And, although man's body is made of clay, he is not simply part of nature: He is made in God's image. Especially in its Western form, Christianity is the most anthropocentric religion the world has seen.[1]

Now I cannot enter here into a discussion of whether White is entirely correct in his description of what Christianity has taught; but it is certainly true that I have met or read about Christians who hold more or less the view of the world that White outlines, and who have come to hold as a result a quite instrumentalist and pragmatic view of the rest of creation in relation to themselves. White himself identifies as a spokesman for this Christian tradition. [Late President] Ronald Reagan when he was Governor of California said of one of the great outstanding features of his state, "When you've seen one redwood tree, you've seen them all." Some Christians, we must admit, hold a view of Christian faith that does not have much place in it for earth-keeping. But is this true of the biblical story that allegedly informs the Christian worldview? Far from it!

Beings in Creation Each Have Their Own Purpose

In the first place, although it is true that Genesis 1 describes the fashioning of human beings as a crucial moment of creation, this does *not* of itself simply mean that "no item in the physical creation had any purpose save to serve man's purposes." One of the recurring refrains of Genesis 1, in fact, is that all creatures were created "according to their kinds"—distinct from each other, in an ordered environment. As Gordon Wenham puts it in his Genesis commentary, "There is a givenness about time and space which God has ordered by his own decree."[2] This "givenness" is all part of the "goodness" of things, and it implies a God-given usefulness and dignity in the case of each individual member of the various families of creation—including plants and trees—that is not dependent upon human beings, even though humans have their own role to play within the cosmos. All creatures are *God's* creatures, whatever their "kinds," and the story of God does not simply involve humans, as Job discovers at the end of his long dispute with God in [the Book of] Job 38-41 where he learns just how far that story concerns non-human creation, and how little it revolves around *him*. Indeed, human beings are themselves resolutely *part* of the creation in Genesis 1 and 2. They do not have a day of creation to themselves, but share the sixth day with the other land creatures. The emphasis lies on the commonality that exists between the humans and the rest of the animal creation. Genesis 2 underlines this commonality, by telling us that humans are indeed "produced" from the earth in the same way as the other animals (Genesis 2:7, 19). Humans are humus. We are made out of soil, "from the dust of the ground," and given life by God who breathes into us the breath of life) (Hebrew: *nismat hayyim*, 2:7). In these respects, we are no different from the other animals. Genesis 1:20 uses the same phrase, "living being," of the sea creatures and 2:19 uses it of the land animals and birds, while 7:22 speaks of the flood as destroying everything that had the breath of life in its nostrils (Hebrew: *nismat-ruach hayyim*). Notice further Psalm 104:30—"When you send your Spirit, they [i.e., all creatures] are created, and you renew the face of the earth." Human beings, in Genesis 2, are only one subset of God's "living beings," into whom God has breathed the breath of life, and they are just as fragile as all those creatures are. They have a limited period of life, and they are vulnerable to threats on every side (Psalm 104:29; Job 34:14). Metaphors of dust and grass most frequently describe them (e.g., Genesis 2; Job 4:19; Psalm 103:13-17). We are wonderfully created as humans, then, but no more so than other creatures. In none of this material would we find a foundation for White's claim that "no item in the physical creation had any purpose save to serve man's purposes." Created beings all have their own purposes and destinies under God, biblically-speaking, independently of their relationships with humans, as a psalm like Psalm 104 beautifully reminds us:

> God makes springs pour water into the ravines; it flows between the mountains. They give water to all the beasts of the field; the wild donkeys quench their thirst. The birds of the air nest by the waters; they sing among the branches. God waters the mountains from his upper chambers; the earth is satisfied by the fruit of his work. He makes grass grow for the cattle, and plants for man to cultivate—bringing forth food from the earth; wine that gladdens the heart of man, oil to make his face shine, and bread that sustains his heart . . . The moon marks off the seasons, and the sun knows when to go down. You bring darkness, it becomes night, and all the beasts of the forest prowl. The lions roar for their prey and seek their food from God. The sun rises, and they steal away; they return and lie down in their dens. Then man goes out to his work, to his labor until evening. (verses 10-23)

The Bible itself, then, does not appear supportive of White's alleged "Christian axiom that nature has no reason for existence save to serve man."[3] The conclusion to the creation week in Genesis 1:1-2:4 occurs, indeed, not on the sixth day with the creation of human beings, but on the seventh when God "rested." It is this Sabbath rest, not the creation of humanity, which completes creation and brings its days to the perfect biblical number of seven. This Sabbath rest was later observed weekly in Israel, on which day it was again the *commonality* of all creatures that was emphasized, not the utility of some in respect of others (Exodus 20:8-11):

Remember the Sabbath day by keeping it holy. Six days you shall labor and do all your work, but the seventh day is a Sabbath to the Lord your God. On it you shall not do any work, neither you, nor your son or daughter, nor your manservant or maidservant, *nor your animals*, nor the alien within your gates. For in six days the Lord made the heavens and the earth, the sea, and all that is in them, but he rested on the seventh day. Therefore, the Lord blessed the Sabbath day and made it holy.

The Cosmos Was Not Created for Human Benefit

What are we to make, secondly, of the notion that "God planned all of this [creation] explicitly for man's benefit and rule?" A non-human being might have its own purpose, but yet at the same time have a purpose beyond that, and higher than that, in terms of serving the needs of human beings. Here we must first of all deal with two of White's other statements, which are somewhat misleading—at least if we are tempted to confuse what the Bible actually says with what some Christians have made it say historically.

"Naming" Does Not Imply Exerting Authority

White states "Man named all the animals, thus establishing his dominance over them." It cannot be established from Genesis 2, however, that the naming of the animals has anything to do with establishing dominance over them. Although the naming of someone in the Old Testament is in fact often done by a person who has authority over another (e.g., a parent), it should be obvious that we cannot deduce from this fact that there is an intrinsic link between naming and asserting authority. The case of Hagar's naming of God in Genesis 16:13 stands as an evident counter-example: "She gave this name to the Lord who spoke to her: 'You are the God who sees me.'" Furthermore, the context of the naming of the animals in Genesis tells against any idea of authority being exercised in this *particular* naming. At this point in the story, a search is being made among the other creatures that God has made to see if any of these is suitable as the kind of soul-mate required by "the earthling"—*'adam* made from *'adamah*, "ground." These are creatures in many ways like the earthling—"living creatures," as we have seen, who themselves derive from the ground (*'adamah*, Genesis 2:7 and 2:19). Many of these derive, like the earthling, from the sixth day of creation. There is a commonality between human and animal creation which at least suggests the possibility that Adam *might* find his deepest needs and aspirations for society among these other animals. The emphasis of the passage lies on kinship and community. I see nothing in it that implies that the naming has anything to do with asserting authority. It is just that the earthling is the one who possesses language, like God.

The Bearers of the Image of God Are Not Transcendent Over Nature

This brings me directly to the second of White's statements that I want to comment on: "Although man's body is made of clay, he is not simply part of nature; he is made in God's image." He goes on to say that "Man shares, in great measure, God's transcendence of nature," and to suggest that it is this belief in human transcendence that has led on to our modern sense of superiority over nature, our contempt for it, and our willingness to exploit it.[4] To this I would only say that if this is what interpreters of the book of Genesis have deduced from it, then they have not been very careful readers of the book; and/or they have perhaps not been sufficiently careful, when reading, to allow the text to critique whichever version of Greek philosophy has been *influencing* their reading at the time. Genesis does not encourage us for a moment to believe that our human status as beings made in God's image results in our not being truly part of nature, but somehow transcendent over it. In Genesis, it is as resolutely mortal, creation-bound persons that we are *also* God's image-bearers. No part of us is "naturally" transcendent, in the sense that it is immortal and divine. It is true that Greek-influenced Christians throughout the ages have spoken in ways that have suggested otherwise, passing down through the ages a dualism of soul and body in which there is a clear distinction between the earthbound and the heavenbound. It is true that this anthropology can all too easily be conscripted to serve in an overall theology of Gnostic [The Gnostics were a group that believed in the utter dualism of body and spirit, so much that they affirmed that there were two Gods—a "lower" creator God who made the earth, and a "higher" redeemer God above nature—and they affirmed that human beings were composites of a "lower" (inferior) body and a "higher" (superior) soul. Because of this dualism, they believed that God would not/could not assume flesh; thus, the Incarnation—God entering the material realm—did not occur/*could* not occur, and Jesus' humanity was only an appearance, an illusion] tendency that is dismissive of the earthly sphere as only the temporary prison of the precious divine "spark" that is destined to fly back to God. The Hebrew Genesis, on the other hand, holds that humans are created by God as *whole* people. The human being of Genesis 2:7 does not *have* a soul, but rather *is* a soul (Genesis 2:7—*nephesh hayyah*, "a living being"); he/she is not a collection of "parts," some heavenly and some earthly, but an *integral* being. This is why Christians, when they are thinking rightly and remembering that they are not Greek philosophers, believe in the resurrection of the body, rather than simply in the survival of the soul—although right thinking about bodies has not necessarily been a defining activity of the Church throughout all the ages!

Now clearly human beings, while certainly not "sharing, in great measure, God's transcendence of nature" as White would have it, from a biblical point of view *are* made in the "image and likeness" of God (Genesis 1:27). We *do* resemble God in some ways that other creatures do not, and various suggestions have been made about what it is that we might share that thus makes us somewhat "divine"—reason, perhaps, or personality, or free-will, or self-consciousness, or intelligence. But as important as any of these aspects of humanness might be as reflections of God's nature and character, they must not be allowed to overshadow what is certainly an important implication of the "image and likeness" language here, which is that human beings are created to be *representatives* of God on earth. That is to say: As important as it is to understand what the language of image and likeness means in terms of our *nature* as human beings, it is just as important to understand what it means in terms of our *vocation*. In the ancient world, kings placed statues (images) of themselves in chosen territories in order to lay claim to that territory—the statue represented the king in his claim to sovereignty over the territory. The king himself, in the common oriental view, was made *in the divine image* as God's representative on earth— both Egyptian and Assyrian texts describe the king as the image of God in this way. This is a particular example of the more general ancient Near East thinking that the images of gods placed in temples were representations of them— mediators of their person and presence. Genesis 2:7 in fact clearly recalls in the mind of the reader who has read Genesis 1 the ceremonies of the ancient Near East that invested such "images" with divine "life" and *enabled* them to function as representations of the gods in their temples. In Genesis, the human creature is formed from the ground out of the clay and shaped and fashioned by God, who then breathes the breath of life into his creation and sets it in a garden by a river. This echoes texts from outside Israel in which we read about representations of the gods being endowed with life by the priests, informed by them that they were to join Ea, father of the gods, in celestial splendor, and led forth by them to a garden by the river to symbolize their new power. The presence of the deity in the statue was magically effected through a ceremony called the "Opening of the Mouth." It is not as autonomous beings that humans are "made in God's image and likeness," then, but as mediators of God's person and presence to the rest of creation. Humans function as representative, delegated government. Such persons, we assume, would only be justified in adopting, as White puts it, a superior attitude in respect of nature, or in expressing contempt for it, or in exploiting it, if this were in line with the will of God who delegated to the person that government; but that does not appear to be the kind of God we are dealing with in the Bible.

Human Rule, But Not Sole Human Benefit

This brings us back to consider, then, White's statement that "God planned all of this [creation] explicitly for man's benefit and rule." It is undeniable that in Genesis 1:26-28 human beings *are* told to rule and to subdue the rest of creation—they are presented as kings within their domain.[5] The verb for "rule" in Genesis 1:26 and 1:28 is *radah*, and it is allied in 1:28 with *kabash*, "trample," "subdue." These are both verbs which echo the Old Testament language about kingship and military conquest. *Kabash* is used elsewhere in the Old Testament to mean "to enslave" (Jeremiah 34:11), "to rape/sexually assault" (Esther 7:8), "to trample underfoot" (Zechariah 9:15). We read of the land (Hebrew: *'erets*, the word used for "earth" in Genesis 1:28) actually being "subdued" before God and/or his people in Numbers 32:22, 29 and Joshua 18:1; and we hear of David "subduing" all the nations in 2 Samuel 8:11. To use *kabash* is to use the language of conquest, usually military conquest; and of its common consequence, which was enslavement. *Radah* represents the language of government. It is used elsewhere in the Old Testament of kings governing their subjects (e.g., I Kings 4:24); of Israel ruling over those who had previously oppressed them (Isaiah 14:2); of the upright ruling over the wicked (Psalm 49:14); of priests ruling at the direction of the false prophets (Jeremiah 5:31); of shepherds ruling the people (Ezekiel 34:4). It is often associated, as in this last passage, with ideas of force or harshness, and indeed slavery (e.g., in I Kings 5:16, where the officers "ruled over" the forced laborers). The language used of human rule over the earth in Genesis 1, then, is fierce—even disturbingly graphic—language. It is perhaps unsurprising that some have taken it to legitimate aggressive, exploitative, and rapacious human actions with regard to the rest of creation, while others have wondered whether we now need a text rather different from the Genesis text: "Do not fill the earth, be kind to it, and live in harmony with other creatures." However, we must insist here on a basic rule in the interpretation of any text, including biblical texts—that words mean what they mean in a *context*. In the first place, the vocation of kings *in the context of the ancient world* did not involve only ruling and subduing, but also looking after the welfare of their subjects and ensuring justice for all (for an Old Testament illustration of this reality, see Psalm 72). To denote human beings as "kings" over the earth by using the language of kingship to describe them is therefore not of itself to imply that these rulers have permission to exploit and ravage the earth. This is especially the case *in a literary context* where it is made entirely clear that the kingship of which we are thinking when we speak of human rule over the earth is derived from the one God who is alone truly King. As Psalm 24:1 will later say: "The earth is the Lord's, and everything in it." Genesis does not have in view absolute and unfettered power, which can be used as human beings will, with no moral restraint. Humankind's responsibility is rather to exercise "dominion" *on behalf of* the God in whose world they live—a just, peaceable dominion, of the sort that is described for us in a psalm like Psalm 72. Genesis 2 makes it clear what this actually looks like in relation to the rest of creation, when it exegetes "dominion" in terms of earth-keeping. The world is portrayed in that chapter as a garden—an enclosed parkland, in which human beings live in harmony with their kin, the animals, and with God who walks in the garden in the cool of the evening. Here the language noticeably shifts from the language of kings to the language of priests, and we find the earthling placed in God's parkland "to work it and take care of it," literally to "serve it and keep/guard it" (Hebrew: *'abad* and *shamar*). This is religious language, which underlines the importance and sacred nature of the task—it is worship and conservation—and also reminds us of the connection between the garden and the tabernacle or temple. Note in particular Numbers 3:7-8: "They are to perform [*shamar*] duties for God and for the whole community at the Tent of Meeting by doing the work [*'abad*] of the tabernacle. They are to take care of [*shamar*] all the furnishings of the Tent of

Meeting, fulfilling the obligations of the Israelites by doing the work ['*abad*] of the tabernacle."

The dominion given to human beings is evidently not a *lording it over* the rest of creation—it is sacrificial *looking after* creation. It is part of our created-ness in God's image that we should imitate God in his creativity and in his providential care for creatures. This is not to negate the importance of the hard-edged language of Genesis 1. In the course of fulfilling the human vocation, ruling and subduing in a forceful way *will* be required of us, along with caring and tending—there is no romantic view of creation-gardening here, in which planting alone, and without weeding, will suffice. It is, of course, all too easy to allow hard-edged concern for creation to dissipate into the kind of mushy and naïve, often anti-technological sentimentality about "Nature," of the kind that we see more and more around us. "Nature" is not, however, the benevolent deity that many would have us believe she is, as the millions of people who struggle with her all over the world would bitterly testify. It does require governance. Genesis 1 and 2 capture the necessary balance, which is also the balance of just government elsewhere in the Old Testament where human society alone is more in view.

In summation, and in response to Lynn White's critique: God did plan crea-tion with human rule in mind, as an aspect of the human role in creation as im-age-bearer, but the Bible resists the idea that God planned creation "explicitly for man's benefit." On the contrary, the biblical view is that human dominion, rightly exercised, is for the benefit of all creation. The ruling king of Genesis 1 and Psalm 8 is at the same time the priestly servant of Genesis 2, a steward of God's world accountable always and in every respect to the Owner of the Gar-den, the Creator. In the Genesis story itself, our earliest extended picture of what this looks like is provided by Noah, "portrayed as uniquely righteous in 6:9 . . . [and] also the arch-conservationist who built an ark to preserve all kinds of life from being destroyed in the flood."[6]

People-Keeping in the Early Chapters of Genesis

To this point, having allowed Lynn White, Jr., to set the agenda, I have been trying to show how the biblical creation story, far from encouraging a casual or negative attitude towards non-human creation, in fact provides a substantial foundation for what we might call an ecological theology. A loving and all-powerful God has created this cosmos that we inhabit, and our very purpose as we live here is bound up with the care of creation, which belongs to God and not to us. If, as White suggests, Christianity is the most anthropocentric religion the world has seen, it is only so in this sense: That it has a very high view of what human beings are and can achieve, and holds them centrally responsible for how things work out in the world in which they have been placed. This is true of how we treat non-human creation; and, of course, it is equally true of how we treat our fellow human beings. This brings us to the second theme: The theme of people-keeping.

Here, too, I would like to begin with Lynn White, Jr.'s, characterization of Christian faith. "By gradual stages a loving and all-powerful God had created light and darkness, the heavenly bodies, the earth and its plants, animals, birds, and fishes. Finally, God had created Adam and, as an afterthought, Eve, to keep man from being lonely." This is indeed a version of Christian faith espoused by some Christians throughout history down into present times. In this version of Christianity, the individual man stands apart not only from non-human creation, but essentially also from that part of human creation that is female. The woman is not intrinsically bound up with the man in terms of the achievement of his destiny any more than the animals are. She merely comes along for the ride to provide the man with some comfort on the way. Some of the Church Fathers even doubted if her company was much to be desired if male company were available instead.

Again, however, we must question whether this view is well-rooted in the biblical creation story. Genesis 1:27 suggests to the contrary that the human beings who are called to the task of exercising dominion over the earth are both male and female. They are both *together* created in the image and likeness of God and jointly commissioned to their task. At the heart of human stewardship of the earth on God's behalf, then, stands human *community*—a cooperating, co-dependent unity. Dominion over the world is not to be exercised by one person, but by humankind corporately in sexual differentiation and togetherness. Nothing is said here of any sequencing in the way that males and females are created, nor of any theological significance that might be derived from such sequencing. Genesis 2 does, then, introduce "sequencing," although it does not make anything of it—which is unsurprising in a section of Genesis where it is generally obvious that the order of events in the creation process is not a pressing concern of the authors.[7] The woman does not "come after" the man in this story (if indeed it is appropriate to refer to the *'adam* creature prior to 2:22 as a "man," since no sexual differentiation has yet taken place in the story), but the important point to notice is that the "man" himself is not yet a properly-created human being in 2:7-20, but only becomes so with the creation of the woman. When God finished each of the days of creation in Genesis 1, and completed the making of all the individual elements of each day, he saw that everything was "good"—including the creation of *'adam*, "human beings." In Genesis 2:18, however, we find *'adam* in a state of "not good": "It is not good for the man to be alone. I will make a helper suitable for him." Human beings are *intrinsically* both male and female—that is the reality that is "good." It is a communal reality. It is the human nature that humans are social beings. In Genesis 2:18 we are not yet there. And when we do get there in Genesis 2:22-23, we find the name first used to refer to the earthling (*'adam*) throughout the story is different than the word for "man" (*'ish*) that is used in verse 23, when the man is spoken of in relation to the woman (*'ishah*). The close similarity of these nouns underlines the close connection between the persons, who are indeed to consider themselves as "one flesh" (Genesis 2:24), in a figurative sense sharing the same body. An "afterthought" the woman is not.

The model used to envision human community in this passage is, of course, marriage; but we find here only a particular expression of a more general biblical view that at the heart of the created order when it is functioning properly stands, not a just human individual, but a just human society. People-keeping and earth-keeping walk hand-in-hand, and the people-keeping is characterized not by hierarchy, but by mutuality—mutually just and loving relationships, in which the nature of the "other" as God's image-bearer is taken deeply seriously. This is a radical, important idea in the context of the ancient world in which the Genesis story was first told. In the ideology of the ancient Near East in general, it was kings and kings alone (with occasional exceptions) who were said to be made in the divine image. The focal point of the language appears to be Egypt, where, beginning with the New Kingdom, there are numerous examples of the king described as the image of a particular god. The pharaoh was described in these terms because he was believed to be the earthly manifestation of the deity, and thus he functioned on earth exactly as the image functioned in the temple. Other human beings, in standard Near Eastern mythology, were created as the servants of the gods to keep them supplied with food. In the Atrahasis Epic of Old Babylon, for example, we are told that "the toil of the gods was great, the work was heavy, the distress was much," so the gods invented humanity to do the work. Ancient Near Eastern culture was therefore resolutely hierarchical, and ordinary human beings were very much subordinate to the kings and their nobles as well as to the gods more generally. They were gods on earth, as their inscriptions often tell us. Contrary to this ideology, Genesis 1 claims that all human beings, indeed both male and female human beings, are made in God's image. There is ruling and subduing to be done, as kings often do in their kingdoms, but it is the ruling and subduing of creation by human beings in general. We have in Genesis, then, the democratization of an older and different idea leading to the apparently uniquely Israelite notion that all persons, not just the king, occupy a preeminent place in the created order. Moreover, human beings are not created for the benefit of the gods in Genesis 1, and certainly not to supply the gods—including the king—with food. Rather, God provides food for all his creatures, including his human creatures—an abundant supply of food that implicitly enables rest from labor once a week on the Sabbath. The dignity of every human person is thus established. There are no gods in the created order, except those "images of God" who are, in fact, all human beings. There is only one God and all his human creatures are on the same level in terms of worth and dignity, and in terms of the blessedness of life that they should enjoy under God. This view of human beings involves thus a fundamentally egalitarian, communal view of things which is quite out-of-step with Ancient Near East ideology and much political and religious ideology since. The various ways in which it is out-of-step are apparent already in the remainder of the Old Testament story, as we shall shortly see.

Earth-keeping and people-keeping, characterized by mutual love and justice, walk hand- in-hand in Genesis. The integral connection between the two is signaled clearly in Genesis chapter 3 and subsequent chapters where dysfunction enters into the human relationships as a result of the human attempt to exercise moral autonomy in respect of God. The man and the woman enter into a struggle for dominance and one of their children murders his brother. Human society spirals downwards morally from this point onwards even as it develops economically and culturally; injustice rather than justice rules. The earth has been a blessed place hitherto, now cursing enters the scene. One result is that the work in the garden, which is already an aspect of the human vocation, comes to involve more pain than it had before; for the ground is cursed by God (Genesis 3:17-19), and this means that much harder work will now be required to grow enough of edible plants to survive. Dysfunction in the human community leads to dysfunction in the relationship between human beings and non-human creation. Ultimately, in Genesis 6, we find the earth "corrupt"—ruined, spoiled— and filled with violence instead of being filled with God's creatures (Genesis 6:11; cf. Genesis 1:22, 28). God "sees" that "all flesh" has in fact corrupted their ways (6:12)—and by "all flesh" is meant humans *and* animals.[8] The point is not that the animals themselves are morally accountable. Rather, animal creation is caught up in the corruption, because where there is human dysfunction there is also dysfunction in the whole organic system that is creation. The consequence is that a great Flood will "ruin" the earth [Hebrew: *shachat*, New International Version "destroy" in Genesis 6:13] which has already been "ruined" by its inhabitants (Hebrew: *shachat* three times in verses 11-12, New International Version's "corrupt/corrupted"). There will be an "uncreation," as the waters positioned within their boundaries by God at the beginning of time break back into the inhabited areas of the earth. Noah and his extended family are spared, however, along with animal-creation-in-miniature and a covenant is eventually made (Genesis 9:8-17) which again involves not only the *human* survivors but "all life on the earth." We could not have a more graphic illustration of the biblical conviction that a human society in which it is not acknowledged that I *am* my brother's keeper (Genesis 4:9) cannot stand and that in its falling it brings down the rest of creation that depends upon it for governance. People-keeping and earth-keeping go hand in hand.

People-Keeping and Earth-Keeping in Ancient Israel

To this point, I have largely confined myself to what the book of Genesis has to say about these two themes and their connectedness. As we move towards the conclusion, however, I should like to say a few words about how these themes play out in the remainder of the Old Testament, as we turn from the story of creation to the story of Israel—with which nation, the Bible teaches us, God's plans in the world were directly bound up for a considerable part of human history. It was in Israel that the truth about God and the world was to be kept alive until the Messiah should come and the cosmos should be redeemed. Israelite society was to reflect, as much as it *could* given the reality of its situation in the ancient, fallen world, just people-keeping and earth-keeping. As a nation, Israel itself had experienced at its birth in Egypt the counter-vision of the cosmos as it was legitimated by Near Eastern mythology in its ancient context. They had suffered under a "god" and had been required to work endlessly for that pharaoh-god as his slaves—a deity regarded in Egyptian religion as responsible for the fertility and well-being of his land, yet suffering horrendous ecological disaster in the plagues of Egypt as a result of his refusal to acknowledge the true and living God. It was in Egypt that Israel was considered in the biblical tradition to have come to know the Lord in fundamentally important ways, sharpened, perhaps, by way of contrast. It is the memory of being slaves in Egypt that seems to inform so much of biblical ethics. In Deuteronomy 17:14-20, for example, we find some guidelines in respect of kingship in Israel, should it ever come about. We notice in this passage a firm emphasis upon the indigenous character of such a king—he needs to be someone who understands Israelite tradition from the inside and who understands therefore that an Israelite king cannot function like an Egyptian pharaoh. We note further that he must be obedient to God's law, particularly so that his heart may not be lifted up above his brethren—he is not allowed to become arrogant, either in respect of his neighbors or in respect of God. He is a commoner-king, not a king of the Egyptian sort; a king who serves as much as he rules. So it is that in the Old Testament vision of true kingship, we find the primary emphasis lying upon the provision of justice, especially for the weak and vulnerable, as in the opening verses of Psalm 72:

> Endow the king with your justice, O God, the royal son with your righteousness. He will judge your people in righteousness, your afflicted ones with justice. The mountains will bring prosperity to the people, the hills the fruit of righteousness. He will defend the afflicted among the people and save the children of the needy; he will crush the oppressor. (verses 1-4)

It was the kind of king represented by the pharaoh, on the other hand, that true worshippers of the Lord in Israel feared, as the prophet Samuel makes clear in I Samuel 8—a king appointed out of a popular desire to have done with God's kingship and to institute a monarchy that the people could call their own. Such a king, warns Samuel, would organize society around his own needs and once again oppress the people. This was, of course, the kind of king that Israel often had, historically. King Ahab stands as a good example (I Kings 16-22). Here was a king who had lost touch with the true God, embracing the fertility religion of his wife Jezebel. He consequently lost touch with himself and his proper role in society, and brought disaster on Israelite society, symbolized and summed-up in his treatment of Naboth [who owned a vineyard that the king wanted, but would not sell it; so through Queen Jezebel, King Ahab had Naboth falsely accused and stoned to death in order to acquire the vineyard] in I Kings 21. It was not just kings who were capable of this loss of memory and the consequent abuse of their fellow image-bearers. The lament psalms [a category of psalms based on a particular structure and with the common theme of grief and protest] are full of complaints about the ways in which the wicked generally oppress people. Psalm 73:4-9 graphically describes their lives:

> They have no struggles; their bodies are healthy and strong. They are free from the burdens common to man; they are not plagued by human ills. Therefore pride is their necklace; they clothe themselves with violence. From their callous hearts comes iniquity; the evil conceits of their minds know no limits. They scoff, and speak with malice; in their arrogance they threaten oppression. Their mouths lay claim to heaven, and their tongues take possession of the earth.

The responsibility that *all* persons have to love their neighbor as themselves, conversely, is everywhere assumed in the Old Testament. It is explicitly stated in Leviticus 19:18, in the context of a number of examples of what this might mean:

> When you reap the harvest of your land, do not reap to the very edges of your field or gather the gleanings of your harvest. Do not go over your vineyard a second time or pick up the grapes that have fallen. Leave them for the poor and the alien. I am the Lord your God. Do not steal. Do not lie. Do not deceive one another. Do not swear falsely by my name and so profane the name of your God. I am the Lord. Do not defraud your neighbor or rob him. Do not hold back the wages of a hired man overnight. Do not curse the deaf or put a stumbling block in front of the blind, but fear your God. I am the Lord. Do not pervert justice; do not show partiality to the poor or favoritism to the great, but judge your neighbor fairly. Do not go about spreading slander among your people. Do not do anything that endangers your neighbor's life. I am the Lord. Do not hate your brother in your heart. Rebuke your neighbor frankly so you will not share in his guilt. Do not seek revenge or bear a grudge against one of your people, but love your neighbor as yourself. I am the Lord. (verses 10-18)

Implicit in all this is the idea that your neighbor is, like yourself, an image-bearer—a person created by the same God as you. In Job 31:13-15, this is explicit:

> If I have denied justice to my menservants and maidservants when they had a grievance against me, what will I do when God confronts me? What will I answer when called to account? Did not he who made me in the womb make them? Did not the same one form us both within our mothers?

In Job's society, there is social hierarchy—there are masters and there are slaves. Yet Job still recognizes a moral imperative towards justice in respect of his slaves, because in the end each of them is, as he is, a person created by God.

One of the things bound up with this "keeping people" in ancient Israel was the issue of how land was dealt with. If our biblical texts regard the earth as a whole as being the Lord's (Psalm 24:1), it is equally true that they regard the small part of the earth occupied by Israel in the same way. This land, too, was a gift from God—not something that Israel owned by inalienable right, because of her own activity in possessing it (e.g., Deuteronomy 8:7-10; 11:10-12; 26:9), and certainly not something earned through virtue (9:4-5). It was something that could be lost if the nation of Israel failed to act justly within it (e.g., Hosea 12:9; Amos 7:17). More than this, injustice itself—human communal dysfunction—is regarded in the prophets as intrinsically involving trouble for the rest of creation. Hosea 4:1-3 starkly describes the entire, ailing reality of Israel in the 8th century BCE:

> There is no faithfulness, no love, no acknowledgment of God in the land. There is only cursing, lying, and murder, stealing, and adultery; they break all bounds, and bloodshed follows bloodshed. Because of this, the land mourns, and all who live in it waste away; the beasts of the field and the birds of the air and the fish of the sea are dying.

Communal dysfunction impacts the land itself, disabling earth-keepers from keeping it properly. One reason is that human violence can directly impact the land. Deuteronomy 20:19, for example, recognizes the way in which war, even in ancient times, was disastrous for the rest of creation, and urges combatants to try to limit the damage—partly for pragmatic reasons, but partly just because trees, in this case, do not deserve to be caught up in the conflict:

> When you lay siege to a city for a long time, fighting against it to capture it, do not destroy its trees by putting an ax to them, because you can eat their fruit. Do not cut them down. Are the trees of the field people, that you should besiege them?

Another reason that communal dysfunction impacts the land itself is that it distorts the relationship between earth-keepers and the earth, placing it disproportionately in the hands of those who do not care for God's laws and certainly do not accept that "the land is mine and you are only tenants" (Leviticus 25:23). The land is a gift of God that has been by God's command distributed equitably to the people of Israel (Joshua 13-22). It is a basic principle in the Old Testament that land is in fact to stay with the family to whom it has been given (Leviticus 25:23-24). Various rules about the redemption of land exist to ensure that this is so (as illustrated, for example, in the Book of Ruth). As we saw in Leviticus 19, there are also rules about allowing the poor to benefit from the land, because they, too, have a part in it. That such a view of things was often set aside in ancient Israel by those who stood to gain most from doing so is evidenced by such passages as Isaiah 5:8-10 ("Woe to you who add house to house and join field to field till no space is left and you live alone in the land"), and Micah 2:1-5 ("They cover fields and seize them, and houses, and take them. They defraud a man of his home, a fellowman of his inheritance"). The Book of Micah in particular paints a stark picture of systemic societal dysfunction in the Israel of his day, as wealth was being accumulated in the hands of a few with the support not only of the judicial system but also of the religious authorities. God is not interested in religion that acts as a cloak for deceit and a comfort for those embroiled in injustice and oppression, claims Micah, even if it is orthodox and conservative religion, or indeed, we might add, evangelical religion. As Micah 6:6-8 famously muses,

> With what shall I come before the Lord and bow down before the exalted God? Shall I come before him with burnt offerings, with calves a year old? Will the Lord be pleased with thousands of rams, with ten thousand rivers of oil? Shall I offer my firstborn for my transgression, the fruit of my body for the sin of my soul? He has showed you, O man, what is good. What does the Lord require of you? To act justly and to love mercy and to walk humbly with your God.

It is more than a great pity—it is indeed a scandalous thing—that this Old Testament "ethics of the land" has so often been spiritualized away in the Christian ethics of our modern period, to such an extent that it is not easy for many modern Christians to understand the kind of easy connection made by Micah in his preaching between religion and social justice, between private morality and social responsibility. To the extent that this disconnect exists, there is a gulf fixed not only between the Bible and its modern readers, but also between these modern readers and Christians of earlier generations like Bishop Ambrose of Milan:

> When you give to the poor, you give not of your own, but simply return what is his, for you have usurped that which is common and has been given for the common use of all. The land belongs to all, not to the rich; and yet those who are deprived of its use are many more than those who enjoy it.[9]

> The world has been made for all, and a few of you rich try to keep it for yourselves. For not only the ownership of the land, but even the sky, the air, and the sea, a few rich people claim for themselves . . . Do the angels divide the space in heaven, as you do when you set up property marks on earth?[10]

Conclusion

Much more could be said. I hope that I have said enough, however, to communicate the way in which the Old Testament looks at the whole matter of people-keeping and earth-keeping. You and I are made in the image of God. We have responsibility to look after other image-bearers; we also have a responsibility to look after the garden in which we have been set. "A Just Faith for a Whole World" involves taking both aspects of our vocation seriously. The Old Testament well understands that in a fallen world it is difficult, for all sorts of reasons, to fulfill either aspect of our vocation perfectly, and indeed to fulfill both of them at the same time. Yet it holds both before us and does not allow us to make easy choices between them. We are to live, indeed, in anticipation of a time when not only *human* society will be ordered perfectly justly, but *the entire cosmos* will be redeemed—the time of a new natural order, indeed of a new heavens and a new earth (Isaiah 27:1; 65:17-18; 66:22; Ezekiel 47:1-12), when "the wolf will live with the lamb, the leopard will lie down with the goat. . . . They will neither harm nor destroy on all my holy mountain, for the earth will be full of the knowledge of the Lord as the waters cover the sea" (Isaiah 11:6-9)—the time of the ultimate fulfillment of the words of Hosea 2:18:

> In that day I will make a covenant for them with the beasts of the field and the birds of the air and the creatures that move along the ground. Bow and sword and battle I will abolish from the land, so that all may lie down in safety.

It is this time that the apostle Paul has in mind in Romans 8:19-22, when he writes of creation waiting "in eager expectation for the sons of God to be revealed," so that these sons of God can do their job of earth-keeping properly and "the creation itself will be liberated from its bondage to decay." In the meantime, our own task is not only to be light, illuminating the darkness of contemporary human society with respect to its true vocation, but also salt, slowing down and perhaps even preventing further creation-decay. People-keeping and earth-keeping are not different options. They are both part of the same Christian calling.

Notes

1 This essay was conveniently reproduced in Ian G. Barbour, ed., *Western Man and Environmental Ethics* (Reading: Addison-Wesley, 1973), 18-30. The quote is taken from p. 25.

2 Gordan J. Wenham, *Genesis 1-15*, Word Bible Commentary (Waco: Word Books, 1987), 21.

3 White, "Ecologic Crisis," 29.

4 *Ibid.*, 25.

5 Psalm 8 further says that humans, having been created a little lower than the angels, are crowned with glory and made to rule the works of God's hand.

6 Wenham, *op. cit.*, 33.

7 Whatever the significance of the fact that the creation of the woman is mentioned after the creation of *'adam* in chapter 2, no interpretation of this fact which is not consistent with the basic thrust of Genesis 1:27-31 can be defended—at least, not if one is interested in reading Genesis 1 and 2 together . . . The mere fact that the woman apparently comes "after" the man of itself cannot be said to prove anything in particular about the importance of the man vis-à-vis the women, nor about the authority that the man is alleged to have over the woman, since *'adam* itself comes last in the chain of creation in Genesis 1 and is formed out of the ground in Genesis 2, and yet *'adam* is not said on that basis to be less important than the rest of creation or indeed subordinate to it.

8 This is contrary to the interpretation found in the New International Version's translation of Genesis 6:12, which renders "all flesh" as "all the people"; cf. Genesis 6:19; 7:16; 8:17; and 9:16 for "all flesh" as referring to both humans and animals.

9 Ambrose, *De Nabuthe Jez. 53*, quoted in Justo L. Gonzales, *Faith and Wealth: A History of Early Christian Ideas on the Origin, Significance and Use of Money* (New York: Harper and Row, 1990), 191.

10 Abrose, *De Nabuthe Jez. 11*, quoted Gonzales, *op. cit.*, 191.

Introduction to article by Clifford Chalmers Cain

In this article, Cliff Cain identifies the various perspectives or ways of seeing nature that originated in the ancient world and that have persisted to the present time. He analyzes the model of dominion in Genesis 1 and the model of service in Genesis 2. In order to understand these seemingly-contradictory emphases, he examines the historical, political, social, economic, and religious contexts in which, from which, and to which these scriptural texts respectively functioned, emerged, and spoke. He maintains that only by keeping these textual emphases in creative tension with one another can the proper balance be attained and maintained in regard to human relationship with the natural world.

He notes that at times the manipulation of matter is justified and required. The cheerleader of control is Francis Bacon, the father of modern science.

At other times, he notes that serving the physical world is justified and required. The patron saint of care is Chief Seattle, the Native American who sought rapport with the land.

But how might these two actions be kept in creative tension? Dr. Cain concludes by introducing the artistic metaphor as one image of stewardship which "could serve as a fulcrum for achieving such a balance and an anchor for such a balancing act."

Stewardship as a Work of Art

Clifford Chalmers Cain

A story about Michelangelo circulated around my Art History class during undergraduate days: When asked how he sculpted such beautiful statues, Michelangelo was said to have replied, "I just chip away everything that doesn't look like it belongs." At the time, and as a person profoundly un-gifted in the fine arts, I thought to myself, "easy for *him* to say!" For to me, it is a magical—even miraculous—event when an artist brings forth almost as a midwife the beautiful or provocative form that lies within the substance of the artist's medium. If the product of the artist's labor was a statue, then that particular shape was residing there in the material all along, and the artist worked delicately and creatively with that medium to allow what was naturally present to come to full, concrete expression.

This sense of relationship between humans and the material world did not begin with Michelangelo. It goes back at least as far as the philosopher Plato. Some philosophers and environmentalists have criticized, and justly so, Plato's bifurcation of reality into the World of Becoming (the realm of matter, things that change) and the World of Being (the realm of Ideas or Forms, things that do not change) and his subsequent valuation of the latter and devaluation of the former. Be that as it may, Plato also believed that there was a Craftsman, a Demiurge, a divine Artist who worked with matter to fashion it into something orderly, beautiful, and harmonious. Indeed, those things in the material world were imperfect and temporal reflections, in a sense, concrete embodiments, of the Ideas or Forms which were perfect and eternal.

Accordingly, for Plato, human beings have as their responsibility the imitation of the Craftsman or divine Artist. As humans work in and with nature's material, they should have as their goal the shaping of the physical world into some semblance of order, harmony, and beauty. Insofar as humans are successful in this, they are cooperating with—duplicating, albeit in an inevitable, less exemplary fashion—the activity of the Demiurge.

As a result, while one might find incongruous the building of the Parthenon on the Acropolis in Athens with the devaluation of matter in the first point in Plato's philosophy, one finds little surprise that such spectacular architectural wonders were created as the consequence of the second point in Plato's philosophy.

For the artist, and for the human who would imitate the Craftsman, there is necessary tension between preservation and alteration. What should be changed, and what must be left as it is? What may be removed, and how much can be "chipped away" before the proverbial "baby" is "thrown-out with the bathwater?" How might the manipulation of matter be performed in such a way that the beauty, order, and harmony that is present within it can be manifested through human involvement rather than be destroyed though human interference?

In the Judeo-Christian tradition, Genesis 1 accents one particular model for the interaction between humans and natural matter—domination. Although some biblical scholars and theologians have attempted to soften the customary English-language meaning of the terms, "dominion" and "subdue" (verses 26 and 28), by suggesting that they are precursors—even euphemisms—to the "kinder, gentler" language of Genesis 2 ("till" and "tend"), this is not warranted by the meaning of the terms in their original Hebrew. The Hebrew word translated "have dominion" is *radah*. *Radah* is used in 1 Kings 9:23 to describe Solomon's overseers levying the forced labor needed to build the Jerusalem Temple, a seven-year project, and his own palace, a thirteen-year program. *Radah* is also used in Isaiah 14:2 of Israel's defeating her oppressors and turning the tables on them. "Have dominion," then, as a translation of *radah*, means to "lord it over" someone or something. Biblical scholar Gerhard von Rad points out that *radah* is also a word used in regard to the wine press and in that context means "tread" or "trample."

The Hebrew word translated "subdue" is *kabash*, which means to "stomp on" or to "trample on." *Kabash* is used in Zechariah 9:15 to refer to Israel's walking on—stomping and trampling—the soldiers of her defeated nation-foes. *Kabash* is used in Jeremiah 34:11 to describe the officials of Jerusalem grabbing back their slaves after having released them during the Babylonian invasion of Judah. And *kabash* can mean rape, when used in a context involving women. "Subdue," then, as a translation of *kabash*, means to "subjugate," "conquer," "beat up," even "rape."

The meaning of "dominion" and "subdue" refers to an aggressive, objectified, instrumental, exploitative relationship between humans and the natural world. And since God set-up the terms of this relationship, it appears that humans' trampling and stomping on the physical world are both divinely-commanded and divinely-sanctioned. Here there is no accent on the intrinsic worth of the material world, but rather on that world's extrinsic or instrumental worth to humans. What use is the world to us? Whatever use we wish to make of it! Matter exists for our sake, not for its own sake.

A number of years ago, Christian and social historian, Lynn White, Jr., picked up on this and charged Christianity with promoting a subjugative relationship between humans and nature and, as a result, with responsibility for the environmental crisis:

> Especially in its Western form, Christianity is the most anthropocentric religion the world has ever seen. Christianity . . . insisted that it is God's will that [human beings] exploit nature for [their] proper ends. . . . Nature has no reason for existence save to serve [humanity].

But, in order to understand the content of Genesis 1, the context of Genesis 1 must be understood: Compiled two centuries or so before Plato recorded his thoughts in the *Timaeus*, Genesis 1 emerged from a specific religious, historical context. The Israelites were in exile in Babylon following the defeat of Judah by King Nebuchadnezzar. Because they were given a certain measure of social freedom in Babylon, the situation was not repressive in either social or economic ways. In fact, several Israelites rose to positions of economic and political power. The most serious concern, however, was a religious one. Israelite faith had centered on the gift of the land (Palestine) and the presumed inviolability of the Temple in Jerusalem, and now these two religious foundations had been lost. And, further, because of the cultural richness of Babylonian society—both in terms of agriculture and industry *and* religious vitality and architecture—there was a danger that the faith of the Israelites would be lost to assimilation.

Thus, the pastoral message to this group in exile, cut off from its geographic and architectural religious moorings, is that the Hebrew God is superior to the Babylonian gods including and especially Marduk, the chief deity and a creator god; that this God created all that is, as well as being the Exodus Liberator of the Israelites in history; and that the Israelites are still "somebodies." This latter affirmation is reflected in the strong language of Genesis 1. Words such as "have dominion over" and "subdue the earth" are addressed to a militarily-defeated and religiously-doubting group of exiles. The hope, the intention, is to bolster Israelite ego and save the faith.

By contrast, Genesis 2 elevates "kinder, gentler" language. In verse 15, the tradition elevates a different paradigm of human-nature relationship. God put humans in the Garden to "till" it and to "tend" it. The Hebrew word which is translated "till is *'abad.* The verb *'abad* is closely related to the noun *'ebed,* or servant, and thus means "work" (till) in the sense of "serve." Here there seems to be expected a role of "gardening," of working in and with the physical world. The Hebrew word which is translated "tend" is *shamar,* which means "to keep" or "to protect." The New English Bible suggests "care for" as the meaning of *shamar,* but there is also a sense of "protect" in *shamar,* since *shamar* is used in Genesis 3:24 to speak of the cherubim protecting the Garden by guarding the way to the tree of life.

"Till" and "tend" taken together constitute a divine mandate for humans to work-in and serve, to care-for and protect, the earth which God has created. The physical world is not there for the taking, in order to satisfy simply and entirely humans' wants and desires. Rather, humans have a more subsidiary status, a more egalitarian relationship with the rest of creation. Being uniquely made in God's image, being distinctively "like God," is not emphasized in Genesis 2 as it is in Genesis 1; instead, humans' intimate connectedness to nature is stressed. In a Hebrew play-on-words, Adam is made from the dust ('adam from 'adamah), just like the animals (Gen 2:7; 2:19). And in case the point is missed, the story of the Fall is placed in the subsequent chapter to illustrate God's judgment on pride.

The context of Genesis 2 further amplifies this point in its content: Genesis 2:4b-25 is a creation account older than Genesis 1 and has been dated in the tenth century B.C.E. It was during this period that Israel ascended to new heights of economic prosperity, human culture, and military power. Indeed, Israel had risen from relative obscurity to the status of a small empire which commanded the political attention and economic envy of surrounding nations. Though King David rightly deserved much of the credit for this rise in fortune and prestige, his son, Solomon, continued, stabilized, and upgraded the policies of his father. Through political savvy, international diplomacy, and strategic marriages, Solomon was able to ensure peace throughout most of his reign, expand trade, enhance the arts, upgrade military capability, and accomplish an impressive building program. The consequence of this was a period of dazzling material prosperity. And the name of Solomon came to be the symbol of the wealth and glory of the empire.

However, with wealth, success, and military might came arrogance, presumed self-sufficiency, and an exaltation of human status. This displeased God, and the prophet Ahijah announced that God would take away the kingdom from Solomon (1 Kings 11:29-39), leaving only the tribe of Judah under the rule of a Davidic descendant. Indeed, for this inflated pride and snobbish self-reliance "the Lord was angry with Solomon" (1 Kings 11:9; cf. 9:1-9), even to the point of raising-up adversaries against him (1 Kings 11:14, 23). When pride shoves aside the awareness of humans' dependence upon God, when people rebel and cast-off their reliance upon God's grace and goodness, God pronounces judgment. Human pride, whether displayed symbolically in the eating of forbidden fruit (Gen. 3) or the building of a mighty tower (Gen. 11), must be punctured, and proper humility encouraged. Thus, whereas Genesis 1 is intended to bolster the egos and save the faith of exiles in Babylon, Genesis 2 is intended to deflate human ego and put persons in their proper place before God.

These images of human relationship to nature (creation) seem to be contradictory—to "dominate" on one hand (Gen. 1) and to "serve" (Gen. 2) on the other. And since "stewardship" appears to be the theological way that the tradition has understood the earth-human relationship, what shape would these rudimentary texts for understanding humans as operational in the world and these foundational texts for stewardship take? Is stewardship the meticulous management of natural resources with an eye only to human benefit; is stewardship a euphemism for domination? Or is stewardship the "putting primary" of nature with humans in a serving, auxiliary role; is stewardship a euphemism for "earth first"?

At times it would seem that the "manipulation" of matter is justified. Indeed, the advances of technology are traceable directly to the intent to master nature. Francis Bacon (1561-1626) is perhaps the patron saint of this intention. Facing the ravages of diseases such as the bubonic plague, he borrowed language from the witch trials of his day to describe a new image of the relationship between humans and nature: Nature would be "put to the question." Only by forcing nature to disclose "her" (this pronoun is consonant with his understanding of nature and connectional with the witch trials) secrets could control over matter be established, disease eradicated, and progress achieved. This control led to developments in science such as the invention of the microscope and telescope, the discovery of calculus, and the emergence of new sciences.

Of course, technology has not been entirely a blessing. Technology has cursed us with intended, unintended, unforeseen, even unimaginable, consequences. The development of the combustion engine incredibly aided industry, transportation, and agriculture. At the same time, the pollution which has come from combustion engine emissions is poisoning the atmosphere at such a rate that natural cycles have been interrupted, even usurped.

The introduction of antibiotics, such as penicillin, revolutionized medicine and our human capacity to recover from infections and diseases. As the parent of two children, I am grateful for the availability of such microbe-exterminating miracles. However, the blessing of antibiotics has been accompanied by a curse. By overprescribing antibiotics and by using the same kind of antibiotics repeatedly, a new generation of antibiotic-resistant bacteria has emerged.

The lesson is clear and challenging: Unless the manipulation of matter is carefully planned, scrutinized in regard to consequences, and seen within its wider ecological context, there can be life-threatening disruptions in the cycles of nature and very dangerous natural consequences. The notion of "dominion" in Genesis 1 must be informed and tempered by the emphasis and message of Genesis 2.

Alternately, at times it would seem that "serving" the physical world is justified. The biodiversity of planet earth is imperiled to an alarming degree: It is estimated that every year between 18,000 and 73,000 animal and plant species become extinct largely because of habitat destruction. By the middle of this century, one-quarter of all species may be lost. Humans in a "caring for, protecting mode" would not only be concerned about these species' extinction, but would also be working to take steps to counter it.

Another example is the problem of deforestation. Trees are being cut-down at an unprecedented rate: Every minute, 100 acres of tropical forest are destroyed. Since the advent of agriculture, about thirty-three percent of the world's forests has been cleared. The United States and Africa have both lost about one-third of their forests, while Brazil, the Philippines, and Europe have lost forty percent, fifty percent, and over seventy percent, respectively. Forty-two million acres of tropical rain forests—the equivalent of the size of the State of Washington—are leveled every year.

Though the United States' timber industry provides employment for a significant number of workers, and lumber products boost the national economy, Christians who take seriously the biblical mandate to "till and tend" the earth would be considering ways of reducing such a rate of harvest and ways of guaranteeing that replanting was proceeding at a much more commensurate and sustainable speed. Concomitant with these actions would be the establishment of job re-training for persons whose economic livelihood was thereby affected.

A third example is the problem of overpopulation. The velocity of population explosion becomes marked when the time span required for adding one billion persons to the world's population is specified. At the time of the birth of Christ, there were two hundred and fifty million persons in the world. World population reached its first billion level in 1850. The second billion took only eighty years (1930). The third billion mark was hit in 1960, requiring only thirty years. The fourth billion took seventeen years (1977), and the fifth billion was reached in 1988, an eleven-year interval, and the six billionth person was born on October 12th, 1999 (according to the United Nations), again an eleven-year interval. Every decade approximately one billion persons are added to the world's population!

Human beings in a creation-caring disposition realize that overpopulation is one of the greatest ecological, biological, global problems which the world family faces. And in this regard, the numbers of persons comprising families would be limited, no matter how many children would be preferred for whatever reason, in order for the resources of the earth to sustain them. This means putting human priorities second and earth priorities first—although the two, of course, are interconnected, for the situation of the ecosystem impacts and affects the quality of human life.

However, though it could be and has been successfully argued that the balance between "domination" and "service" has been historically tipped in favor of the former at the expense of the latter, an alternative, compensatory, one-sided emphasis on "earth first!" ignores the fact that nature is not benign. The same physical world that offers such beauty as the sunsets in the Caribbean, the bright blue feathers of the blue jay outside my study window as I write these words, and that inspires such wonder and awe as photosynthesis and the carbon cycle, the constellations on a clear summer's night, the cross-pollination of plants, the biological harmony and physiological complexity of the human body, threatens us with cancer, hepatitis, and Alzheimer's, with tornadoes, floods, and earthquakes, with AIDS, ebola, and SIDS.

Once again, it would seem that a dynamic, creative tension or balance between dominating and serving, between altering and preserving, between manipulating and caring-for, is indispensable.

Images or metaphors are crucial for bringing this to concrete expression. How a reality is regarded, how a role or responsibility is perceived, provides the context, and a springboard, for action. Depending on one's "way of conceptualizing" something, certain forms of behavior will be either endorsed or prohibited. Philosopher Michael Novak uses the term "horizon" to refer to these specific ways of "seeing."

Social ethicist Gibson Winter discusses "paradigms" or "root metaphors" in the same way Novak speaks of "horizons." Paradigms or root metaphors emerge from the experience of persons living in the world. Or better, paradigms are drawn out of a people's experience of its world—these paradigms or metaphors organize thought and experience and in so doing provide a basis for action. In doing so, they are the generators of meaning, for they guide our making sense of the world in which we live. For example, regarding the world as a machine furnishes coherence in a person's interpretation of nature, life, and the world. So does a perspective on the world as an organic unity. Both provide contexts and impetuses for action—the former for the manipulation and control of a world organized by systems of calculation; the latter for solidarity and participation in a world organized around the rhythms of life and nature.

These two root metaphors, horizons, images, or ways of "seeing"—the mechanistic view and the organic view—parallel Genesis 1 and 2. The mechanistic metaphor puts humans "above" the natural world in a position of/for mastery and domination. Creative power is to be used to transform matter. This also is reminiscent of the artist's urge to alter the medium in which he or she is working.

The organic metaphor places humans "in" nature in a position of solidarity and participation. Bonding and attachment are drawn-upon to maintain the integrity of things as they are. This also is reminiscent of the artist's urge to preserve the medium in which she or he is working.

Francis Bacon would be an appropriate cheerleader for the mechanistic metaphor; a Native American like Chief Seattle would be an appropriate patron saint for the organic metaphor.

Of course, some balance must be sought which will hold in dynamic, dialectical tension the creativity and the continuity, the alteration and the preservation. Is there a way in which "stewardship" can maintain a combination of the "hard" language of Genesis 1 with its emphasis on power, and the "soft" language of Genesis 2 with its concern for the land? Is it possible to think of upholding both emphases in such a way that creative balance is given to both sides? And if so, what image or metaphor could serve as a fulcrum for achieving such a balance and as an anchor for such a balancing act?

The "artistic metaphor" is one which appeals to several religious thinkers. It is not a perfect metaphor, and it does not settle everything, but it does provide a way of bringing together the steward's manipulating and maintaining functions in order both to transform and to preserve. For the artist's task is both to alter and to conserve.

Theologian George Hendry argues that the work of the artist is as close to the divine act of creation as anything human gets. Of course, the artist works with matter that she or he did not create; nevertheless, the artist provides form, order, and draws out the beauty contained within that material. The art thusly-created points to a bridge, a connectedness between the artist and the work of art.

Artists speak of a kind of conversation between the medium and the artist. Hendry calls it "communication." If the artist manipulates the material as a puppeteer dominates a puppet, then the creative process is a "monologue," rather than a "dialogue." The tension between changing and maintaining is crucial to the mutual relationship between artist and material. And this tension is maintained by a two-way communication.

The steward who would maintain the balance between alteration and preservation must listen to the creation. What is nature saying to him/her? What is known, and can be further learned, about the rhythms, cycles, "laws," and lessons of nature? How could something be done in such a way as not to violate the integrity, harmony, and beauty of nature? How may the creation be lovingly shaped so that life is enhanced rather than harmed?

The biblical image of the potter and the clay seems *apropos* here: In Isaiah and Paul, the potter displays absolute power (dominion) over the clay. But in Jeremiah 18:1-11, when the prophet enters the potter's shop to observe the craftsman at his work, he observes that there is a kind of "conversation" going on between the clay and the potter. Indeed, the clay protests to the potter about what he had done to/with it. In this scenario, the clay is not a worthless object which is being shaped and contorted into something which violates its very "suchness." Instead, the artist and the clay are "cooperating" in bringing forth something that is pleasing and creative, something that preserves the integrity and interests of both parties. Here the clay is more of a "subject" than an objectified "it."

Philosopher John Dewey emphasizes an "aesthetic-artistic process" in the coming to be of an artistic work. At each step in the emergence of the work, aesthetic sensibility and artistic creativity interplay and mutually influence each other. Just as with the potter and the clay image, there is a dual "movement" in true creativity, for the human artist is receptive in his or her active creativity, and creative and active in her or his receptivity. If the artist is attuned to (receives) the "message" from matter and has his or her sights set on creativity enriching human experience and meaning without violating the sanctity of the substance involved, then, in Paul Klee's vision, "the human is productive and receptive at once, only becoming truly creative through its receptivity." This dynamic relationship between "attunement" and "modification" points to a servant or mid-wife image for humans. The resultant bringing-forth or letting come forth points to the fact that "this [kind of] congruity of nature and the human species makes art possible."

Stewardship as a work of art, as artistic process, provides a metaphor which helps to keep in dynamic tension, supplies a fulcrum which strives to keep in balance:

> alteration and preservation
> power over and solidarity with

creativity and continuity
manipulation and maintenance
transformation and participation
modification and attunement
productivity and receptivity
change and conservation
control and restraint
domination and service.

Introduction to article by Elizabeth Theokritoff

In this article by a prominent Orthodox theologian, the reader will find a rich contribution from the resources of the Eastern Christian tradition *and* a reminder for the entire tradition of some of the meanings of concepts, terms, and insights held in-common. For instance, Dr. Theokritoff's treatment of "repentance" at the end of the article is particularly helpful and essential to prompting and effecting the changes that are necessary in attitude and action in a world of increasing environmental degradation and pollution; for a "change of heart" connects both the spiritual and the material.

In addition, and throughout, she rightly asserts a theocentric perspective—that is, that the world is neither to be polluted nor worshipped. The first action is a violation of the sacredness of the world *because God is present in it*. The second is a violation of the Christian obligation to worship *only God*: Invoking the image of the icon, so central to Orthodox devotion and theology, she asserts that one may love the world, but not as an end in itself; one must love the world as "transparent to God."

[THE ORTHODOX CHURCH AND THE ENVIRONMENTAL MOVEMENT: Original version published in Alexander Belopopsky and Dimitri Oikonomou, eds, *Orthodoxy and Ecology Resource Book* (Bialystok: Syndesmos, 1996). A slightly amended version was published in *Sourozh* 58 (November 1994) pp. 13-27. Present revised version © Elizabeth Theokritoff, 2008.]

The Orthodox Church and the Environmental Movement

Elizabeth Theokritoff

Author's note: This paper was originally written for a seminar on Orthodox Youth and Ecology in 1994. Much has changed since then, and the question to which my original paper was responding, 'What are we to make of the environmental movement?', has long since been displaced by 'How do we respond to the environmental threats that confront us?' That, indeed, is a question that many Orthodox writers have addressed in the intervening years—some of this work is represented in the appended bibliography. Here, I have left the structure of the 1994 article intact, trying only to modify some passages which might otherwise give a distorted picture of the contemporary Orthodox approach to environmental issues.

The engagement of the Orthodox Church with environmental issues must be one of the most positive things that have happened in the past few decades. It is something to be eagerly welcomed, not only because of the importance of these issues, but also because what we are seeing here is, potentially at least, very much a two-way process. Increased awareness of the crises facing our world challenges us as Christians to find new ways of living out our faith, and often reminds us painfully how far our own example falls short of the faith we profess. It can take a voice from outside to jolt us into a fuller understanding of our own tradition. Such a voice is provided by those who would define themselves first and foremost as environmentalists, whether they focus on the practicalities of environmental problems or make caring for the earth the cornerstone of a spiritual world view. We need to be open to such voices with great humility. But at the same time, the shared experience of threats to the very earth we all live in provides so many opportunities for a witness to our Orthodox faith, to the message of life and hope in the Saviour who so loved the world that He became part of His own creation. I want to look here at some of the areas in which, according to my limited experience, there seems potential for fruitful interaction between Orthodoxy and the environmental movement. These areas can be loosely gathered under four headings:

1. Man and his environment—a spiritual problem.
2. Do we need to save the earth?
3. In a global village, who is my neighbour?
4. A way forward—or a way back?

There is one point that must be made clear at the outset. The Church does not exist to serve secular ends, even the noblest of secular ends. It cannot serve as a vehicle for putting across the message of the environmental movement, or of any other movement. The Church will always have a different emphasis from any movement or pressure group in this world because it operates on a different scale—not just global, but cosmic. As citizens, many of us will agree that environmental concerns should be at the top of the social and political agenda. But we shall also understand that the Church can never make an issue such as protection of the environment, or social justice, central to its preaching—not because we can live according to the Gospel without these things, but because these are works that will be "added unto us" as we "seek first the Kingdom of Heaven". The importance of these things is incalculable, but it is derivative. For this reason, attempts within the Church to look deeply into our own tradition and see what it entails for our use of the material world are absolutely crucial. They must never be seen as a theological distraction from the "real" task of cleaning up pollution, starting recycling schemes and lobbying politicians to stop building yet more roads. The urgency of the environmental problems must never be allowed to obscure the Church's cosmic perspective (correspondingly, it would be a cynical distortion to suggest that this cosmic perspective is trivialised when we worry about stopping air pollution from the local factory or using recycled paper).

There is a potential danger in love and concern for the earth that we must guard against: Even God's creation—that creation which He looked upon, and saw that it was very good—risks becoming an idol if we cherish it and value it apart from Him. To quote Father Alexander Schmemann:

> Man has loved the world, but as an end in itself and not as transparent to God. . . . The natural dependence of man upon the world was intended to be transformed constantly into communication with God in whom is all life...When we see the world as an end in itself, everything becomes itself a value and consequently loses all value, because only in God is found the mean-

ing (value) of everything, and the world is meaningful only when it is a "sacrament" of God's presence...The world of nature, cut off from the source of life, is a dying world.[1]

Seen in this perspective, the struggle for the mere physical survival of this world marked by the Fall is a pointless exercise, a perpetuation of death. We save a species from extinction—but all the individuals of that species currently alive will be dead in a few years just the same, and the species itself may eventually become extinct anyway. For us, therefore, protection of the environment cannot be merely a desperate attempt to hang onto the status quo, to preserve at all costs a life that is by its nature transitory. No, our love for the frail things of God's material creation makes sense only as a sign—a sign that God comes into His world to give life and not death, and that our appointed task is to preach this good news to all creation. This vitally important difference of perspective should not lead us to be dismissive or suspicious of others who care deeply for the created world. Rather, it reminds us that their care and reverence needs to be taken a step further. It is precisely the Three Children who would not worship the creation rather than the Creator who gives us our model, crying out to the earth and the mountains, the plants, the seas and rivers, sea creatures and birds and all beasts, "All ye works of the Lord, bless the Lord; sing and magnify Him forever."

1. Man and His Environment—A Spiritual Problem

One of the great breakthroughs made by the environmental movement is the recognition that the roots of human destruction of the environment are to be sought not just in actions, but in our most deep-seated attitudes. Certainly, it is possible to look at the environmental crisis largely in utilitarian terms. The ozone hole brings increased risks of skin cancer; polluted rivers and dying fish threaten people's health and livelihood; the destruction of rain forests adds to the build-up of greenhouse gases as well as destroying many plant species that might prove to have medicinal value. But as one thinks seriously even just about man's needs, the basic requirements for survival—breathable air, drinkable water, non-toxic food—keep shading off into other needs, harder to analyse but no less 'real'—for beauty, for space, for contact with the living world around us. And this is already to recognise that man is more than a statistical unit: His welfare cannot be reduced to economics and technology. It is not enough for him to keep alive by consuming the world around him: He needs a relationship with it that is not purely utilitarian and consumptive. It is this relationship that has gone drastically wrong in what are ironically called "developed" societies. Increasing numbers of people are drawn to the conclusion that our destruction of the environment is merely one symptom of a whole set of human attitudes to the rest of nature which are necessarily unsustainable because they are profoundly misguided. (Examples of such attitudes are the ideas that we can alter entire ecosystems with impunity, that the world has value only as "raw material" to be exploited for economic gain, or that a catastrophe for other species will leave us unaffected). And many environmentalists go a step further to see in these attitudes a serious spiritual problem.

The mess we have made of the world, then, has forced on many people a recognition that we are not the all-powerful masters of the laws of nature: We are creatures, part of the created world, and we cannot treat the rest of the world as if it is our property to use however we like. A belated recognition, to put it in theological terms, that the promise "You shall not surely die . . . you shall be gods," (Gen. 3:5) is a snare and a delusion. This would not have been a revelation to many people before the "Enlightenment" and the Industrial Revolution; but for the modem industrialised world, it is an amazing reversal. This is an opening which we must be prepared to seize, preaching the truth both of man's creatureliness, and of his unique God-given responsibility for the whole of material creation. One way that other Christians are trying to do this is by inventing new forms of worship that "affirm" material creation. I do not believe that we have any need to do this; but we do need to make an effort to understand, and to show to others, the full implications of the way that our Church tradition already experiences the world as a vehicle for God's grace, transparent to Him.

The quest for a new environment ethic, with its radical rethinking of man's place in the world, has the potential to be a truly providential opportunity for Orthodox witness to today's world. But we shall not be able to make use of this opportunity unless we realise the obstacles that have to be tackled first.

To put it bluntly, many people concerned about the environment see the Christian tradition as the source, not of the solution, but of the problem. In its most extreme form, this line of argument actually sees the root of the present crisis in the supposed "license for exploitation" provided by the commandment to "Fill the earth and subdue it, and have dominion over every living thing" (Gen. 1:28). This suggestion has been refuted often enough, with profound and detailed explanations of what this mandate does and does not mean in the Christian understanding. Here, I want to underline only that there is a serious historical objection to this negative interpretation of the Christian tradition. If exploitation is built into the Christian understanding of man's relationship with the rest of nature, it is very hard to explain why a Christian civilization with the expertise and sophistication to build Agia Sophia [the famous, beautiful church in Constantinople—now Istanbul, Turkey—built by Emperor Justinian in 537 A.D.] or invent Greek fire should have totally failed to develop exploitative technologies or policies as we know them today. Far from having its origins in the heyday of Christian civilization, the exploitative mentality seems to have gained currency only after the "Enlightenment," which marks the decline of the Christian influence on the way people looked at themselves and their place in the world.

Another variant of this argument discounts Christianity as the possible source of an environmental ethic on the grounds that it is "anthropocentric". The following summary of the views of an American lecturer in ethics is typical: "Judeo-Christian anthropocentrism must open up to a spiritual sense of our place in nature and of earth as the sacred work of the Creator;" and it continues, "at present, we find it nearly impossible to grasp that we live in a world that we did not create and cannot control." The assumptions about cause and effect here deserve some comment. Failure to understand that we live in a world that we did not create and cannot control is undoubtedly central to our current environmental problems. But it is not easy to make a convincing link between this dangerous misconception, and belief in a God who challenges man, "Where were you when I laid the foundations to the Earth? Tell me, if you have understanding . . . Have you commanded the morning since your days began . . . do you give the horse his might . . . is it by your wisdom that the hawk soars, and spreads his wings towards the south?" (Job 38:4, 12, 16; 39:19, 26). Obviously, from the Christian point of view, the idea that man is in ultimate control of the world is possible only if you leave God out of the picture. Central to the Christian understanding of the world is not man, but God. It is in Him, the Master and Creator of all, that we relate to each other and to all the other creatures that He has made. It is in His image that we have dominion over all other living creatures. Indeed, the ancient Syriac translation of the relevant verse in Genesis (1:26) makes the connection crystal clear by saying, "Let us make man in our image, after our likeness, *in order that* they may have authority. . ."[2]

Whatever "dominion" we have is in the image of God, the God who is "King forever" and "has wrought salvation in the midst of the earth"—which means on the Cross, in the ultimate humility of His death for the life of the world. Certainly the teaching of the image of God in man gives man a high dignity, as well as a commensurate responsibility. So that if one tries to distil from Christianity a "world view" or theory of man's place in nature without reference to God, the result is likely to look "anthropocentric." But such a "world view" is no longer the Christian faith. The Christian faith is not actually designed, so to speak, to make sense apart from God.

Given the frequency with which the charge of "anthropocentrism" is made, it is hardly surprising that a number of Christians have accepted it and feel the need to apologise for it. I would suggest that, rather than apologise for the undoubted place of honour that we ascribe to man, we should be prepared to defend it and to explain why it is not to the detriment of the rest of creation. Christianity certainly stresses the special position of man in relation to God and to the rest of creation. This contrasts with religions that are considered, in some quarters, more "environmentally sound"—such as those that identify certain animals with divine spirits, or that teach the reincarnation of the soul in various other creatures.

There are two aspects of the Christian view of man that I want to comment on here. Firstly, man is seen as uniquely placed to manifest and mediate the praise of God from the rest of the natural world. In the words of Leontius of Cyprus:

> Through all creation visible and invisible, I offer veneration to the Creator
> and Master and Maker of all things. For the creation does not venerate the Mas-

ter directly and by itself, but it is through me that the heavens declare the glory of God . . . through me the waters and showers of rain, the dews and all creation, venerate God and give Him glory.[3]

This is not to deny that there is a real link between God and His non-human creation. On the contrary, if the potential for praising God were not built into the very structure of created things, we should not be able to manifest it. In fact, what we have is a kind of synergy of created beings—all creation bears the stamp of God's glory, but by His economy it is given to man to bring this potential to its fulfilment. Adherents of other religions—or none—may disagree with this evaluation of man's place in creation: But a license for exploitation it certainly is not. On the contrary, this understanding of man's responsibility seriously circumscribes the ways in which he can legitimately use material creation. In its high assessment of man's role, it embodies a realism which can best be understood from the negative side. What I mean is this: Man's crucial role as mediator becomes tragically clear when we see his unparalleled capacity to obscure the glory of God in nature, to drown God's handiwork under the debris of his own greed and arrogance.

Secondly, the teaching about man in general has always been balanced in the tradition of the Church by teaching about man in particular—that is, our neighbour. This does not exclude showing neighbourliness also to other creatures—we may recall the story of St. Sergius of Radonezh giving his last piece of bread to a bear, because it could not be expected to understand the meaning of fasting. But it might well exclude, for instance, telling a famished traveller that there was nothing to eat because the bear had prior claim. This stress on the importance of man, not as an abstract entity but in the person of the brother or sister standing in front of us, is something that we must insist on. It may be able to serve as a much-needed bridge between the human suffering of people whose immediate basic needs—for food, fuel or livelihood—conflict with the interest of the environment, and an environmental agenda that is often perceived as putting their welfare some way behind that of whales, tigers, or rosy periwinkles. This perception of conservationist priorities is often less than fair, and sometimes due to deliberate misrepresentation—but it can cause great bitterness and polarisation. We recognise, certainly, that radical disruption of the natural environment is in no one's ultimate interests. But any approach that sacrifices the person to the principle, seeing other human beings as inevitable casualties for the sake of a greater good, will be profoundly alien to Christians.

Awareness of the spiritual dimension of the environment crisis, coupled with a reluctance in some quarters to take the Christian tradition as a basis for an environment ethic, creates a dangerous vacuum. This vacuum is filled all too often by eastern religions or by a "New Age" synthesis of religious and spiritual beliefs ranging from earth-mother worship to reincarnation to divination with crystals. Let me be perfectly clear: There are large numbers of environmentalists who have no sympathy whatsoever for this kind of spirituality. But the danger it poses is twofold. On the one hand, it leads some people to see any concern with the environment as neo-paganism and nature worship, and therefore a threat to our faith. On the other hand, New Age spirituality, with its very prominent emphasis on respect for the earth and all its creatures, can actually seem an obvious and attractive option for environmentally-aware people looking for a spiritual home. The tragic irony of the situation is this: So many of the elements that people value in the New Age movements—harmony of man with nature, a sense of the sacred permeating creation, the dignity of the material world—are so richly represented in the authentic Christian tradition, if only people had ever really encountered it. This is all the more reason for us to recall that it was to a pagan world that St. Paul preached the identity of the Unknown God, and to take up his example.

2. Do We Need to Save the Earth?

If we are looking for points of contact with the environmental movement, we may well start by noting the prevailing terminology. Today, instead of hearing about "developing" or improving our natural environment, or even "protecting" it, we increasingly hear about *saving*—the whale, or the rain forests, or the earth itself. Of course, "to save" means many things, not necessarily closely connected with salvation in a theological sense. But all senses of saving have one thing in common—the implication that the situation is desperate. Commenting on the meaning of salvation, Fr. Alexander Schmemann writes: "A drowning man, a man whose home is engulfed in flames, a man falling over the edge of a cliff does not pray for comfort or comforting words, but for salvation." And yet, he continues, " . . . we have stopped viewing ourselves as beings who are truly perishing, beings whose life is rushing inexorably towards meaningless collapse"[4]

The interesting thing to note is that this is probably rather less true today than when it was written a few decades ago. "Meaningless collapse" is a fate that we can very easily envisage for the whole of our civilisation and for earth itself as a viable habitat for ourselves and many other creatures; and the fact that this will come about, if it does, through our own fault, raises the question of salvation from the power of death in acute form. This is the point at which the Church should be offering its own view of what we have to do to "save the earth". Compared with the view of most secular environmentalists, the task as we see it will be at once more radical and less formidable.

For us, what the earth requires (along with all of creation) is indeed salvation in the fullest sense. It does not need simply to be relieved from the worst depredations of human poverty or greed and allowed to regulate its own climate and ecosystems without interference: It needs to be "set free from bondage to decay and obtain the glorious liberty of the sons of God" (Romans 8:21). To address environmental problems on a purely functional level, without repentance, might if successful ensure the continued survival of humanity and many other species—but it would be doing no more than to control the symptoms of the malaise.

On the other hand, we can confidently affirm that, in a sense, we do not have to save the earth. This is where we can provide a desperately needed message of hope amidst the sense of doom and almost paralysing pessimism that so often characterises warnings about the state of the environment. It is not that these warnings are alarmist—often far from it. But they make us feel dwarfed by the enormity of the problems, the insignificance of any individual's contribution, the weight of complacency and lack of political will—not to mention the agonising conflicts of interest when people's entire way of life is tied in with polluting industries, destructive patterns of agriculture or hunting of threatened species. In human terms, the task seems hopeless—until we realise that *it is not up to us to save the earth.* It is not up to us because the earth, along with all creation, is saved in Christ. Of course this does not mean that we have no responsibility: What I am talking about here is a matter of *synergy.* We are responsible for doing everything in our power to work out that salvation in all our dealings with the world—to work with God's purpose and not contrary to it. But we should be in no doubt that God who made the world out of nothing is able to rescue our planet from the brink of destruction, even when our most careful scientific predictions suggest that the cause is hopeless. The clear understanding that we humans are reaping the consequences of our very own actions should in no way cause us to lose heart—that would be to deny the possibility of repentance and forgiveness. We may recall that in the prayers of the Litya, we implore the Lord "to turn away from us the *righteous* chastisement that impends against us, and have mercy upon us." This basic confidence in God's saving power will not diminish either our sense of urgency, or our dedication to finding ways of undoing human damage to the earth and its creatures. But it does enable us to do all these things, in the words of St. Isaac the Syrian:

> Humbling ourselves always, and giving the glory to Him who works with us in everything and is the cause of our victory; and placing ourselves in His hands in the struggle, saying to God, "Thou art mighty, Lord, and Thine is the struggle. Fight and conquer in it. Lord, on our behalf." Because the power that works with us is never defeated.[5]

If we need to sound a note of alarm for those who are complacent, the note of hope for those who are acutely aware of the environmental crisis is no less timely. Some years ago, I attended an ecumenical meeting on the subject of "creation." One of the speakers, a Protestant theologian, described finding her nine-year-old child one night sleepless and tearful, and wanting to know, "Mummy, can the hole in the ozone layer be repaired?" She went on: "I want my children to know what it is to celebrate . . . to learn that love sometimes involves waste . . ." Indeed, the programmes prescribed even to keep greenhouse gasses and other forms of pollution at current levels can seem an austere and joyless list of prohibitions. But for a very different model, we need only to look at the way we use material things in our liturgical life. The fasts certainly give us an example of a frugal—though by no means joyless—use of resources, schooling us to accept even the simplest of foods with thankfulness. But fasting is only one aspect of liturgical life; we also feast. There are times when we also learn how to give thanks for the abundance of good things, earthly as well as heavenly, that God has bestowed on us—while the awareness that these are always gifts should prevent abundance from leading to contempt. And, yes, love does sometimes involve waste in material terms: We need only think of the mounds of flowers brought to church for Easter, or Holy Friday, or the Exaltation of the Cross. But this lavish use of the world has nothing in common with the waste of resources that accounts for so much of the environmental damage in more affluent societies. The latter sees resources as ours by right, guaranteed to remain freely available as long as we can pay for them. By contrast, when we use flowers and branches to adorn the church we are (or should be) offering something precious back to Him who "opens His hand, and all things are filled with good." When we take first-fruits of the material world not for our own consumption, but to offer them back to God, it is an expression of our confidence that the "rich have become poor and gone hungry; but they that fear that the Lord shall not lack any good thing."

3. In a Global Village, Who Is My Neighbour?

Revelations in recent years of the ways in which humans have affected our environment have made us learn the hard way something that we should know as a basic truth of Christian anthropology: We are members one of another, part of the same body, and what each of us does affects the rest of mankind. Even if we have always tried to live according to this belief, the environmental movement is in large part responsible for giving us a whole range of new examples of what it means in practice. We can now see, not only ways in which our affluence deprives the poor of their basic needs, but ways in which it inflicts on them what they need least of all, such as a toxic landfill or a power station on their doorstep. We are also made increasingly aware of the links between environmental degradation and economic pressures. These may be pressures of poverty, where people have to clear irreplaceable forests in order to grow food for a year or two, or a country is forced into the environmentally devastating monoculture of cash crops to service crippling foreign debts. Or they may be pressures of affluence, where large numbers of people are employed in the manufacture of inessentials, which have to be made less durable and sold to more and more people who don't need them in order to preserve jobs. Either way, we can no longer escape the realisation that each of us plays some part in this complex economic network.

All this raises in a new and acute form the question, "Who is my neighbour?" Once we have the opportunity to learn how even our private choices of food, clothing and goods can benefit or harm people whom we shall never meet, we cannot shrug off our responsibility towards them simply because they live on the opposite side of the world. Avoiding harm to others by my choices can seem so complicated as to be hardly worth attempting, and we certainly cannot all become experts in the intricacies of international trade. But I believe that we can and should take advantage of the information available to us and act on it as best we can—not in a doctrinaire way, such as by boycotting certain products on principle whatever the awkwardness caused to our immediate neighbour, but as an expression of love and care for the neighbour whose life touches ours only indirectly. To dictate positions that should be taken in economic affairs is not the role of the Church—but to encourage awareness of the consequences of our actions is surely a legitimate exercise. When in many ways we are acutely conscious of living in a "global village," it is not honest to dismiss this awareness of our place in a global economic network as "meddling in politics" and imagine that we can be responsible only towards those with whom we are in daily personal contact.

As we learn more about the effects of our actions on others, we must expect to be challenged to live out our faith in new ways. Perhaps the most striking example of this is the question of population. We can learn very little about the pressures on our environment before realising that virtually every problem is exacerbated by the weight of human numbers. Activities that have been largely sustainable for millennia, such as small-scale farming, become destructive when there is no longer enough suitable land to go round. If we bear in mind that the *increase* in world population between 1950 and 1970 was approximately twice the estimated *total* population of the world in the mid-seventeenth century, we may realise the scale of the problem. Nor is it just a matter of food resources: People also need places to live, energy to keep warm and cook their food, and some sort of livelihood. World hunger and malnutrition might in principle be soluble by more equitable use of existing resources; but the amount of energy available to the world population as a whole is limited both by the finite quantities of most energy sources and by the environmental costs of all major methods of energy production. Let it be quite clear: We are not talking about limiting population for the sake of a materialistic "quality of life" measured in terms of modern conveniences and high-tech gadgets. We are talking about saving millions of people from abject misery. If this is materialistic, it is the same "materialism" as obliges us to feed the hungry and clothe the naked instead of giving them edifying tracts about the unimportance of material things. If we accept this reality, it is hard to avoid the conclusion that one way of furthering this basic work of charity is voluntarily to limit the size of one's own family.

Recognising the effects on others of even so intimate a matter as how many children we have is just one instance of the profound change in thinking that the environmental movement is bringing about among many people in the industrialised world. Understanding the roots of the global crisis spells an end to individualism—a recognition that co-operation, not competition, is the way forward. Nothing of the earth's bounty is "my own." "This cursed and abominable phrase comes from the devil," as Chrysostom says with typical directness, "we cannot say 'my own light, my own sun, my own water'."[6] At the same time, environmental thinking takes us beyond an impersonal collectivism, with the recognition that "small is beautiful" and that problems need locally- appropriate solutions that are on a human scale. Of course, I am not claiming for a moment that either of these aberrations—individualism or collectivism—is dead. On the contrary, the pressure to exploit whatever and whomever one can for profit, coupled with the terrifying power of a few multi-national companies to impose a uniform culture of consumerism on the entire world, has never been a greater threat. But in the environmental movement we find a powerful and articulate ally in the struggle against these tendencies. It provides a climate in which people may be receptive to a model of human society that is in the image of the Holy Trinity— a society of persons in relationship, neither isolated as individuals nor subsumed into a faceless collective. The historically close connection of the Orthodox Church with various national cultures puts the local Churches in a unique position to lead the quest for local solutions to environmental problems.

4. A Way Forward or a Way Back?

There is a wide measure of agreement on the problems the world faces, and on some of the practical steps necessary to alleviate them. But when it comes to principles for guiding a sustainable way of living for the future, the discussion can resemble that of a party of lost travellers at a crossroads: Everyone knows they are going the wrong way, but no one can agree which road to take instead.

At one extreme, there is the thinking that seems to hark back to a golden age when hunter-gatherers killed their prey with respect and had minimal environmental impact (there were fewer of them, which also helped). Of course, nobody imagines that we could all return to such a way of life; but it is seen as a model, along with the nature religions that such cultures often professed. At the other extreme, there are plenty of people for whom the realities of environmental destruction are an unwelcome intrusion into their comfortable way of life, best solved by technologies that allow them to lessen their environmental impact without changing their habits. And in the middle there is the large body of environmentalists who try to combine greater simplicity with "green" and appropriate technologies.

The "back to nature" argument is superficially attractive. There is no doubt that without our ability to manipulate nature, we should not have got ourselves or the world around us into the present mess. It is not simply that we have been motivated by greed or arrogance. Even our most benign interferences with the natural order, such as the eradication or control of childhood diseases, turn out to have some negative consequences for the environment and for its inhabitants. Technological advances at work and labour-saving devices around the house manage to leave us with less, not more, time for the important things of life. They make it even harder to appreciate the worth of the task in hand, whatever it may be: We are constantly encouraged to think only of results, and to want them as quickly and conveniently as possible. Yet we seem to be locked into a cycle of tinkering more and more with the natural order. Even conservationists trying to restore "natural" habitats discover that they cannot just leave everything to nature as if man had never interfered; the most they can do is intervene judiciously to simulate natural conditions. We have created a legacy of destruction that will not go away even if we stop adding to it from this moment; in many cases, it will get worse unless new technologies are devised to ameliorate it. This suggests that the only realistic way out is a way forward. Simplifying our lives is indeed a necessity for those of us in the developed world, and we need to recognise that technology cannot be a substitute for real changes in our way of life. But the lessening of our individual demands will have to be coupled with ever more sophisticated ways of counteracting the impact on the earth of the human population as a whole.

When we look at specific instances of new technologies, however, we see that the issues they raise are rarely simple. One of the most striking examples is the genetic manipulation of crops and livestock, which a number of people— some of them genuinely disinterested—hail as an answer to food shortages, scarcity of agricultural land and the dangers of pesticide use. Yet environmentalists and social activists sound repeated warnings about the loss of genetic diversity and the potential for exploitation of small farmers. And underlying these concerns there is often a deep-seated unease that manipulation of nature to this extent crosses some sort of threshold—scientists are "playing God." One can debate whether there really is a clear ethical dividing line between modifying other creatures by genetic engineering or by selective breeding; but from a Christian point of view, this may be to miss the point. Many Church Fathers would remind us that access to the basics of life is God's gift to all his creatures: "He opens his hand, and all things are filled with good" (Psalm 103/4:28, Septuagint). This suggests that whatever means are used, if we try to profit from these basics at others' expense (e.g., by preventing farmers' retaining seed from year to year), or, arguably, if we breed animals incapable of enjoying a normal healthy life, then we are already "playing God" in an important and sinister sense.

Regardless of whether we accept some aspects of biotechnology as legitimate, I would suggest that there is good reason to be profoundly disturbed by the idea of a human reshaping another creature to his own specifications and patenting the result. This process speaks of a culture in which humans have shifted from being creatures of a Creator, albeit ones who bear his image in a unique way, to being the sole conscious creative force. We are seeing the logical consequence of a worldview in which nature has no meaning or purpose—no guiding wisdom—except whatever humans decide to give it. Amidst the fears about disrupting the natural order in potentially catastrophic ways, we might reflect that our creatureliness is a key part of that order.

The Tower of Babel may serve as a parable here. The devastating consequences of many previous scientific "breakthroughs," from DDT to toxic plastics, should be telling us that there is a heavy price to pay if we try to usurp God's role as the wisdom that guides creation.

Does this mean that, after all, the only way out is back? That the attempt to bring technology to bear on environmental problems is illegitimate, and therefore not viable in the long term? The answer, I believe, is no. The inventive and adventurous use of nature by man is not an aberration, but something fundamental to his own nature. If we try to deny that this is an aspect of our God-given nature, of the divine image in us, that will not make it go away. It will only take us down the dangerous road of treating all technology as a necessary evil, unrelated to the process of coming closer to God through his creation. There is no escape from the arduous task of learning how to wield our formidable technical skills with wisdom and humility. And this is essentially what "appropriate technology" consists in: Whether or not it is expressed in these terms, it depends on discerning how God's wisdom is operative in nature so that we work with it rather than against it.

This brings me to my final point. There is a strand in environmentalist thinking that sees the problem as, quite simply, man—a uniquely destructive species destined to ruin everything it touches. It is a small minority who would say this in an explicit and strident way. But conservation strategies often seem to reflect the same underlying view, working on the assumption that the only way to protect some part of the environment is to restrict all normal human activity there. Restricting certain human activities may sometimes be very necessary, particularly when we are dealing with large numbers of potential "users." But we must bear in mind that the Lord put Adam in a garden "to till it and keep it" (Gen. 2:15). He did not put him in a park with strict instructions to picnic in designated areas only and to keep off the grass. Of course, there is a vast and fateful difference between the way we use the world in our fallen state, and what God intended. But this does not invalidate the basic point: Man is a part of the natural order, not as just another animal, but precisely as man—a creature who makes ingenious and creative use of the world around him, and in this way gives glory to God. The "dominion" that is given to him starts with the "beasts" within himself, as St. Gregory of Nyssa makes plain; it is no use ruling over the wild beasts outside while we give free rein to those within us.[7] This defines the sense in which we must indeed find our way "back to nature"—to the true nature of man, who is creative but also created.

Perhaps the greatest gift the Church can give to those who love God's creation and are deeply ashamed of man's part in its destruction is the witness of the Saints—that man can be the means of restoration for the world, not by trying to merge in with other animals and leaving no mark on the world, but by becoming more fully human. There are few better ways to express this truth than by pointing to the icon—that extraordinarily audacious use of elements of the material world combined by human artifice to become transparent to God. In the words of Bishop Basil (Osborne) of Sergievo:

> The icon bears witness to the fact that there is a way back for man . . . that he is not condemned to an ever-increasing estrangement from God or to the creation of an ever more opaque world. There is a corner that can be turned. Man can create forms that help God to be present in this world.[8]

***

It would be no exaggeration to say that the message of the environmental movement is a call to repentance. To be sure, this "repentance" begins as a change of heart for the sake of survival. But there is no reason why it should not prepare the way for us and others to heed the message to repent and believe in the Gospel. The connection between the two sorts of "change of heart" is further apparent when we look at monastic communities: Dedicated to a life of repentance, they are so often drawn to a "green" way of living and treating their surroundings, without even thinking of it as "environmentalism." Much more could be said about such examples within the Church.[9] If I have instead spent time on aspects of the environmental movement which may be disturbing to some Orthodox, it is because these need to be confronted and dealt with openly; they must not be left as an excuse for some people to dismiss "environmentalism" as a New Age heresy only superficially congruous with Orthodox Christianity. Given the environmental threats that confront us today, I do not believe that concern for God's material creation can be confined to a discrete group of "Orthodox environmentalists." I believe it is one of the most vital ways in which we are called to bear witness today to our faith in the living Saviour of the world.

For further reading:

John Chryssavgis, *Beyond the Shattered Image* (Minneapolis: Light and Life Publishing, 1999).

Ignatius IV, Patriarch of Antioch, "Three Sermons: A Theology of Creation; A Spirituality of the Creation; The Responsibility of Christians," *Sourozh* 38 (Nov 1989), 1-14.

Bishop Kallistos of Diokleia, *Through the Creation to the Creator* (Pallis Memorial Lecture 1995; publ. *Friends of the Centre*, London 1996).

Anestis Keselopoulos, *Man and the Environment: A Study of St Symeon the New Theologian* (Crestwood: St Vladimir's Seminary Press, 2001).

Fr. Dumitru Staniloae, "The Foundation of Christian Responsibility in the World: The Dialogue of God and Man," in A.M. Allchin, ed., *The Tradition of Life* (London: Fellowship of St Alban and St Sergius, 1971), 53-73.

Elizabeth Theokritoff, "From Sacramental Life to Sacramental Living", *Greek Orthodox Theological Review* 44:1-4 (1999), 505-524.

"God's Creation as a Theme of Missionary Witness; An Orthodox View," in Lukas Vischer (ed.), *Witnessing in the Midst of a Suffering Creation* (Geneva: John Knox Centre, 2007), 115-134.

Notes

1*For the Life of the World* (Crestwood: St. Vladimir's Seminary Press, 1973), 16-17.

2See Sebastian Brock, "Humanity and the Natural World in the Syriac Tradition," *Sobornost/ECR* 12:2 (1990), 131-142.

3Fifth Homily of Christian Apologetic against the Jews, and on the Icons, PG 93:1604B.

4*Celebration of Faith, Sermons, Vol. 1* (Crestwood: St. Vladimir's Seminary Press, 1994), 68-69.

5Hom. 39; *The Ascetical Homilies of St. Isaac the Syrian;* tr. By Holy Transfiguration Monastery (Boston, 1984), 195.

6*On Ephesians* Hom. 20; Catharine P. Roth and John Anderson, tr., *St. John Chrysostom On Marriage and Family Life* (Crestwood: St. Vladimir's Seminary Press, 1986), 62.

7*On "Let Us Make Man . . ."* PG 44; 270D.

8*The Light of Christ* (Oxford: St. Stephen's Press, second edition [revised], 1996), 52.

9See further, Elizabeth Theokritoff, "A Eucharistic and Ascetic Ethos: Orthodox Christianity and the Environment," *Shap Journal: World Religions in Education 2008/2009*, 25-27.

Introduction to article by Seyyed Hossein Nasr

Distinguished Muslim scholar, Seyyed Hossein Nasr, walks us through the impact of secularization on our perception of the natural world. Because we have de-sacralized nature, it is vulnerable to our exploitation and manipulation of it as an array of objects, simply there for our taking.

By contrast, the sacred view of nature sees the natural world as the "theater of Divine Creativity and Presence." That is, the world was created by God, and God remains creatively present in it. As a result, human beings cannot re-sacralize nature; for we do not have the power to "bestow the quality of sacredness upon anything."

What we must do, then, is recall and re-discover the sacred quality of nature. Religion is crucial in this, for not only does it point to the Transcendent, but it also places restraints on human sins such as greed, materialism, and consumerism. Thus, religion can redirect and transform our human activities on earth. The religions of the world—and here he definitely means all faith traditions and not just Islam—have an absolutely essential role to play.

In this regard, he also discusses the power of ritual, anchoring the discussion in Islam but also appealing to similar aspects of other world religions. Ritual can re-assert that the Transcendent is truly what is deserving of worship. Self-worship—and its associated selfishness, narcissism, and permissiveness—is neither permitted nor healthy. Humans can then become the revivers of a sacred view of nature and the guardians (*khalifat Allah* or the "vice-regents of God") of the sacred.

Religion and the Resacralization of Nature

Seyyed Hossein Nasr

Let us cast aside this veil,
Veil of forgetfulness and ignorance.
Let us remember again who we were, are, and shall be,
And what is this world of Nature,
Our complement, our companion, our abode,
Like us the fruit of the fiat lux,
Still bearing within her that morning light,
Light of the dawn of Creation,
And still witness to that wisdom Supreme,
Locus of the Presence of the Realm Divine.
Let us honor her in her sacralized reality,
And not rend her asunder with that voracious aggression,
Which will but erase our life here on Earth,
Divinely ordained as our home of which we are a part.
To honor Nature we must first recall the Source of all,
And seek within, that reality now hidden.
Let us then cast aside the veil,
And remember who we are and what Nature is,
Nature which will have the last word on that final day.
Let us remember and not forget,
Lest we lose the occasion and recollect,
And in destroying Nature our perdition quicken.

We have journeyed long and far through diverse worlds and over many centuries to come to this point of affirmation of the sacred quality of nature, now forgotten and in need of reassertion. Nature needs to be re-sacralized not by man who has no power to bestow the quality of sacredness upon anything, but through the remembrance of what nature is as theater of Divine Creativity and Presence. Nature has been already sacralized by the Sacred Itself, and its resacralization means more than anything else a transformation within man, who has himself lost his Sacred Center, so as to be able to rediscover the Sacred and consequently to behold again nature's sacred quality. And this remembrance and rediscovery can only be achieved through religion in its traditional forms as the repositories of the Sacred and the means of access to it. Furthermore, such a transformation can only come about through the revival of the religious knowledge of the order of nature, which itself means the undoing of the negative effects of all those processes of transformation of man's image of himself, his thought, and the world about him that have characterized the history of the West during the past five centuries. . . .

The history of the modern world is witness to the fact that the type of man who negates the Sacred or Heaven in the name of being a purely earthly creature cannot live in equilibrium with the Earth. It is true that the remaining traditional peoples of the world also contribute to the destruction of their environment, but their actions are usually local and most often the consequence of modern inventions and techniques of foreign origin, whereas the modernized regions of the globe are almost totally responsible for the technologies that make the destruction of nature possible on a vast scale, reaching as far as the higher layers of the atmosphere. It is the secularized worldview that reduces nature to a purely material domain cut off from the world of the Spirit to be plundered at will for what is usually called human welfare, but which really means the illusory satisfaction of a never-ending greed without which consumer society would not exist. There is no escaping the fact that the destruction of the natural order on the scale observable around us today was made possible by a worldview that either had denied or marginalized religion as well as weakened and penetrated it from within, as one sees in the West during the past few centuries and most forcefully in recent decades.

There are those individuals who take recourse to a new philosophy in the current sense to save the natural environment, but such philosophies are not sufficiently powerful to sway the human community on a global scale at this moment of acute crisis. Nor do they have access to the sacred, which alone can enable us to reassert the sacred quality of nature and therefore realize its ultimate value beyond the merely utilitarian. They can certainly help in changing the mental landscape cluttered by so many forms of philosophical agnosticism and nihilism, but they cannot bring about the change in the human condition necessary for even the physical survival of human beings. Only religion and philosophies rooted in religion and intellection are capable of such an undertaking. It might, in fact, be said that, while man lived according to traditional teachings, he was not only at peace with Heaven, but also by virtue of that peace, he lived in harmony with Earth. Modern man, who has eclipsed the religious view of the order of nature and "ghettoized" religion itself, has not only caused the disappearance of numerous plant and animal species and endangered many others, but has nearly caused humans themselves to become an endangered species.

Many people point to the practical and ethical issues involved in the environmental crisis—such as the unbridled greed of present-day society—that have increased by a thousandfold the destruction of the environment, and they have sought solutions only on the practical level. Even if we limit ourselves to the realm of *praxis* [action], however, one must question what power save external brute force can bring about control over the passionate elements within the souls of human beings so that they will not demand so much materially from the world of nature. There might be a few philosophers for whom such a power might be reason, but for the vast majority of human beings it cannot but be relig- ion. The passions within us are like a dragon now unleashed by modern psycho- logical perspectives for which evil has no meaning. Only the lance of a St. George, the lance symbolizing the power of the Spirit, can slay the dragon. How tragic is the world in which the dragon has slain St. George. The passions thus let loose cannot but destroy the world.

Man is created to seek the Absolute and the Infinite. When the Divine Prin- ciple, which is at once absolute and infinite, is denied, the yearning and the search within the human soul nevertheless continue. The result is that, on the one hand, man absolutizes himself of his knowledge of the world in the form of science, and on the other hand he seeks the Infinite in the natural world, which is finite by definition. Rather than contemplating the Infinite in the endless mirrors of the world of Creation that reflect the Divine Attributes and Qualities, man turns to the material world for his infinite thirst, never satisfied with what he has on the material plane, directing an unending source of energy to the natural world with the result that it transforms the order of nature into the chaos and ugliness we observe so painfully today in so many parts of the globe and which bear the mark of modern man's activities. Spiritual creativity is replaced by in- ventive genius, which leaves upon the environment the traces of its unending tinkering with nature and production of gadgets and products in the form of ever-increasing refuse and waste and of the creation of ever-growing wastelands with which the natural environment can barely cope.

Furthermore, this misdirecting of the yearning of the soul for the Infinite to the material world, and the change of the direction of the arrow of progress from that of the soul journeying to God to purely material progress, is made so much more lethal by the absolutization of terrestrial man with its consequent anthro- pomorphism; man and only man is now the measure of all things. In such a situation it is only traditional religions, with their roots sunk in the Divine and their means of directing the soul to its ultimate goal, that can provide a real cure for the illusion of a center-less soul seeking the Infinite in the multiplicity of nature and the Absolute in its circumferential mode of existence. Only religion can discipline the soul to live more ascetically, to accept the virtue of simple living and frugality as ornaments of the soul, and to see such sins as greed for exactly what they are. And only religion, or traditional philosophies drawn from spiritual, metaphysical, and religious sources, can reveal the relativity of man in light of the Divine Principle and not according to that type of relativism so prevalent in the modern world, which seeks to make relative the Absolute and its manifestations in religion in the name of the theory that all is relative, except of course that human judgment which claims that all is relative. Unless man realizes his relativity in light of the Absolute, he is bound to absolutize himself and his opinions no matter how hard he tries to demonstrate an unintelligent humility vis-à-vis the animals and plants or nebulae and molecules.

Religion thus is essential on the practical plane to redirect and transform the activities of man and bestow spiritual significance to the rapport between man and the natural order. This is why so many contemporary religious thinkers concerned with the environmental crisis have turned to the issue of environmental ethics. . . . Yet religious ethics, although necessary, is not sufficient. What is needed in addition is the reassertion of the religious understanding of the order of nature, which involves knowledge and not only ethics. A religious ethics cannot cohabit with a view of the order of nature that radically denies the very premises of religion and that claims for itself a monopoly of the knowledge of the order of nature, at least any knowledge that is significant and is accepted by society as "science." The ground must be cleared and a space created for the reassertion of the religious understanding of the order of nature as authentic knowledge, without denying other modes of knowing nature as long as the latter are kept within the confines imposed upon them by the limitations inherent in their premises, epistemologies [theories of knowledge], and what one would call their boundary conditions, all of which are encompassed in their paradigms.

To use a contemporary term, somewhat overused and maligned, there is need of a paradigm shift. . . . Such a shift would make available a worldview where the religious understanding of the order of nature in the traditional sense would be accepted as authentic along with sciences based on particular dimensions of nature, such as the quantitative, all within a metaphysical whole where in fact each mode of knowledge would be accepted as part of a hierarchy leading to the highest science, which is the science of the Real as such. . . . It is not for us here to talk of the constituents of such a paradigm, which could not but come from the resuscitation of traditional doctrines, nor of the integration of modern science into a universal metaphysical framework, nor even of the future rapport between religion and science. Our aim here is to assert categorically the necessity of the acceptance of the religious view of the order of nature on the level of knowledge, and hence a sacred science rooted in the metaphysical perspective, if a religious ethics involving nature is to have any efficacy. It is also to emphasize the necessity of clearing the ground and opening up an intellectual "space" within the contemporary worldview for the religious knowledge in question to find an abode and to begin to be taken as real and as serious knowledge corresponding to an objective reality rather than being relegated to the subjective, the marginal, and even the occult, with all the dangers that such a situation involves.

Undoing the Effects of the Fall of Man

In the sacred rite of pilgrimage (al-hajj) to the house of God in Makka [or "Mecca"], Muslim pilgrims circumambulate around the Kaaba seven times in a counterclockwise direction opposed to the movement of the arrow of time. The deepest meaning of this aspect of the rite is the undoing of the effects of the Fall of Man and his reintegration into the Edenic state by virtue of which his imperfections and sins are overcome and he regains his state of original purity. One might say figuratively that a similar process has to be undertaken intellectually, mentally, and psychologically in order to reassert seriously the religious knowledge of the order of nature. The processes, both philosophical and scientific, that led not only to the secularization of the cosmos, but also the monopoly of such a view in the mainstream of modern thought in the West, have to be reversed. Contemporary man must be able to reabsorb whatever is positive in the later phases of his mental development, such as certain types of empirical knowledge of nature, back to the origin or to the metaphysical dimension of the traditional religious universe in which the domain of nature still possesses a sacred meaning.

Man must have the negative elements of his immediate past, which are veritable sins, in the theological sense, against the Spirit expiated through the very process of return and reintegration similar to the case of the pilgrim. Moreover, in the same way that the reintegration of the pilgrim into the Edenic state does not imply the loss of his memory or personality, such a return by contemporary thought certainly does not mean forgetting what has been learned, as long as it is real knowledge and not conjecture parading as science. The question is one of integration of the sciences into a metaphysical perspective and, furthermore, the reestablishment of a knowledge of nature rooted in tradition religions . . . as well as the rediscovery of an aspect of nature as reality to which this knowledge corresponds. Only in this way can the religious understanding of the order of nature be reasserted seriously and a reality to which religious ethics corresponds be rediscovered. Anything short of that goal fails to do justice to the meaning of the religious understanding of nature and overlooks the dichotomy between pious assertions of religious ethics such as the sanctity of life and a completely dominant "science of life" for which the very term "sanctity" is meaningless. It also fails to come face-to-face with what underlies the environmental crisis and the forces threatening human existence on Earth.

Even if such a "space" were to be opened up and the religious view of the order of nature reasserted, it would of course have to be of necessity on a scale global in its intellectual outlook although local in its practical applications. The integral teachings of the Western religious tradition must be rediscovered and reformulated beyond the distortions and limitations imposed upon them by five centuries of secularist sciences and philosophies. Moreover, the view of other traditions must also be expounded both for the followers of each tradition and for a global religious perspective on the order of nature that would be able to confront in a united voice those who deny any meaning, purpose, or sacred quality to nature. One might say that the formulation of such a global religious perspective on nature, to which this present study is itself devoted, complements the formulation of the doctrine of the Divine Principle in a universal perspective and across religious frontiers to which those who have spoken of "the transcendent unity of religions" or "global theology" have devoted their efforts.

In the same way that there are many heavens, each belonging to a particular religious cosmos, and yet a single Heaven of which each of the particular heavens is a reflection and yet in essence that Heaven Itself, so are there many earths and forms of religious knowledge of these earths. But there is a perspective that encompasses many salient features of those diverse forms of religious knowledge, despite their differences, leading to a knowledge of *the* Earth that would be recognizable by the various religious traditions at least in their sapiential [wisely discerning] dimensions if not in their theological, social, and juridical formulations. It is in the light of this knowledge, drawn from various traditions—which can in fact enrich other traditions in many ways today—that we must seek to reassert the sacred quality of nature and to speak of its re-sacralization.

It is also in the light of this knowledge that we must appraise whatever significance a particular discovery in physics or some other science might have beyond itself. Modern science *qua* modern science cannot deal with the philosophical and metaphysical implications of its discoveries. And if individual scientists do so, they make such interpretations as philosophers, metaphysicians, and theologians. This assertion remains true as long as modern science functions within its present paradigm. What will happen if there is a change of paradigm is another matter. In any case, such remarkable discoveries as Bell's theorem [the shift from understanding that an event occurring at one place cannot instantaneously affect an event someplace else, to understanding that events *do* affect all other events near and far; this 1964 theorem is sometimes called "non-locality"] cannot themselves lead to metaphysical and theological truths, but have metaphysical implications that could only be comprehended if the religious knowledge of the cosmos and the order of nature as understood in their text were to be accepted as a legitimate mode of knowledge of nature. In any case, such a knowledge is of the utmost significance for the rediscovery of the sacred quality of nature and the re-establishment of a rapport based on harmony between man and nature. It is also crucial for creating a new understanding between religion and science, and, with the help of traditional metaphysics, for integrating modern science into a hierarchy of knowledge wherein it could function without claims of exclusivity and without disrupting the essential relation between man and the cosmos, which possesses a reality beyond the realm of pure quantity and even beyond the empirical and the rational.)

The Religious Cosmos

Beyond the diverse cosmologies and understandings of the order of nature in various traditional religions, there stands, as already mentioned, a religious view of the cosmos that reveals remarkable universality if one goes beyond the world of forms and the external to seek the inner meaning of myths and symbols in different religious universes. First, it needs to be remembered that a religion not only addresses a human collectivity; it also creates a cosmic ambience, a sector of the Universe that shares in the religious realities in question. When a devout Muslim sees the crescent moon at the beginning of the lunar month, he closes his eyes and offers a prayer to God and sees in the moon the symbol of the Islamic revelation and, more specifically, the Prophet, who might be said to possess a "lunar" nature. Buddhists hear the *dharma* [the Buddha's teachings] in the flow of rivers, and for Hindus, the Ganges *is* the river flowing from paradise, the river which, being holy, purifies those who bathe in it. For Judaism and Christianity there is such a thing as the Holy Land, and Jerusalem is cosmically significant precisely because of its nexus to religious events of crucial importance associated with it. Moreover, for traditional Jews and Christians, this significance is not only historical or imposed by human memory, but cosmic. Mt. Sinai is not just any mountain that some human being considers to be important because of the Mosaic revelation. It is important in itself within the universe of Abrahamic monotheisms. Likewise, Spider Rock in Canyon de Chelly, in Arizona, is not only considered sacred by the Navajos; it *is* sacred within their religious cosmos.

This truth is brought out in the cosmological schemes of many traditions, from the Tibetan Buddhist, to the Christian, to the Islamic. The various Buddhas *do* perform many functions within the Buddhist cosmos. Christ and the angels *are* real within the Christian universe, not only subjectively, but also objectively. And the *Mi'raj* [the nocturnal journey of the Prophet] during which he ascended to Heaven from Jerusalem not only in spirit or soul, but also bodily (*jismani*), *did* take place objectively within a cosmos that is Islamic for those who participate in the Islamic revelation. One could multiply examples a thousandfold, especially among primal peoples such as the Australian Aborigines, the tribes of the American Plains or Meso-Americans, but there is no need to do so here. What is important is to become aware of the universality of this principle and its *reality* from the point-of-view of the religious understanding of the order of nature. It is precisely this reality that is now denied in that sector of humanity affected by secularism, scientism, and modernism because in that world the religious knowledge of the order has been deprived of any legitimacy, and the realities forming the object of this knowledge have been either denied or subjectivized and psychologized. A purely quantitative science of nature could obviously not do otherwise. Nor could those philosophers and even theologians who accept that kind of science as the only legitimate knowledge of nature. And yet, the religious view is based upon a truth that cannot be denied once its metaphysical significance is fully understood.

According to the metaphysical teachings of various traditions and the cosmologies which are their applications to the cosmic sector, the Divine Principle is not only the Origin of the cosmos, but also the source of the religion that links humanity to both the Divine Principle and the order of nature. Some religious traditions such as Confucianism, Daoism, and Buddhism do not concern themselves with the creative and generating function of the Divine Principle as do the Abrahamic monotheisms and Hinduism. But in both types of faiths, there is the Supreme Principle that is the Origin of both man and the cosmos, even if "Origin" is not understood in a cosmogonic [the beginning comes to be because of some sort of transcendent Creator] sense in some cases. More particularly, each religion is the manifestation of a Divine Word, a Logos, or demiurgic principle that, within the religious cosmos created by a particular revelation of "heavenly dispensation," is the direct source of the religion in question as well as the immediate "ruler" of the cosmos within which that religion functions.

To use the terminology of the Divine Word or Logos common to the Abrahamic religions, it can be stated on the one hand that God said, "Be (*kun*) and there was" (Qur'an XXXVI:81) or "All things were made by him [the Word or Logos]; and without him was not any thing made that was made" (John 1:3). On the other hand, this Word through which God created the world is in Islam the Qur'an, one of whose names is *Kalam Allah*, the Word of God, and in Christianity, Christ. The source of the very existence of the cosmos and the origin of revelation are therefore the same in each religion. And it is through revelation that the inward nexus between the follower of a particular faith and the "cosmic sector" in which that faith dominates is revealed.

Within each religious universe, the Logos manifests the Divine Reality as well as God's Will and His Grace to the realm of Creation along with the world of men and enables human beings to gain an inner understanding of and a sympathy (in the original Latin sense of *sympatheia*) for the realm of nature . . . Human beings are composed of spirit, soul, and body, all of which are permeated by the grace of the religion in question, and they participate in the divine laws promulgated by that religion. The cosmos is also composed of corresponding levels of existence of which only the most outward, corresponding to our bodies, is discoverable by relying solely upon the external senses. Moreover, in the same way that our body is related to our psyche and soul and our soul to the spirit at the center of our being, even if most of us remain unaware of this link, the external body of the cosmos, permeated like the microcosm by the light and grace of God emanating through the Logos, is also linked to the higher levels of cosmic existence, to what traditional cosmologies describe as "souls of the spheres," "Nature spirits," angels, the World Soul, the cosmic intelligences, and so forth.

Of course, as a result of man's present spiritual imperfection and fall from an original state of purity, he has lost direct access to the Spirit within, to the inner kingdom that Christ asks his followers to seek before everything else. Likewise, the world of nature has been darkened and in a sense participates in man's fall and what Christian theology calls Original Sin. But not having committed the sin of man, nature is more innocent and therefore still preserves more than fallen and imperfect man something of its original and paradisal perfection now finally being destroyed by a humanity that does not even show interest in the meaning of sin, much less man's committing of it and responsibility for the consequences of his actions.

In any case, the reality of the levels of both macrocosmic and microcosmic reality remains, and it is this reality that provides the ontological [pertaining to the way things are] structure for the religious understanding of the order of nature. Within the religious universe, man is related to the world of nature not only through physical elements or even psychological resonances, but through the Logos and ultimately God. Each plant has a significance not only in its physical appearance, but in its subtle reality and ultimately in reflecting and being a symbol of a divine archetype, residing immutably in the Divine Intellect, with which it is identified essentially here and now. A person who has reached the center of his own being sees in every phenomenon of nature, in the crystals, plants, and animals, in the mountains, skies and the seas, realities that are not exhausted by the "merely" physical, but that reveal themselves through the physical, realities that also reside within the being of man and come from the Logos and ultimately God. Man is thus united with nature in body, soul, and spirit and, in the final end, to God. On a more concrete and immediate plane, he is united to the cosmos around him by the Logos who is the immediate origin of the rites and symbols governing his life and the source of the life of the world about him as well as its laws and ultimate meaning.

Furthermore, precisely because man possesses a consciousness and intelligence capable of knowing the Absolute and reflects the Divine in a central manner as a theomorphic [bearing God, in some sense] being, he is also the channel of grace, or what Islam calls *barakah*, for the world of nature. Nature is governed not by man, despite his claims, but by God. And yet it is given to man to act as the bridge (*pontifex*) between Heaven and Earth and as a channel of grace and light for the natural order. That is why his responsibility is so grave. He is given the power to rule over nature, but also the capability to destroy it or bring corruption upon the face of the Earth, against which the Qur'an speaks in many passages [e.g., XXIX:36]. His actions have a cosmic consequence whether he desires it or not, and his abdication from the role of pontifical man to accept the role of Promethean man . . . cannot but affect the order of nature in the most negative way. The denial of the role of the Logos in the cosmos and rejection of a knowledge derived ultimately from the Logos but concerning the cosmos cannot but have the direst consequences for the order of nature and, of course, for man himself, as contemporary history demonstrates so clearly.

Religious Rites and Cosmic Harmony

One of the consequences of the metaphysical doctrine of the meaning of the cosmos and man's role in the religious universe in which he lives is confirmation of the rapport between sacred rites and harmony of the order of nature. As a result of the eclipse of the religious view of nature in the modern world, the very idea that sacred rites might be related to cosmic and natural events is considered preposterous or at best quaint, to be studied by cultural anthropologists as relics of an "animistic" past or made the subject of jokes and caricatures, as in the case of the Native American rain dance. That prayers might actually affect weather conditions, or religious rites influence the course of some natural calamity, are simply not a part of the modernist and scientific worldview even if many individuals today, who still possess faith, continue to pray for a sunny day when they want to plant the fields or climb a mountain. What is denied in the prevalent modern perspective is in fact one of the essential elements of the religious view of the order of nature that is worthy of the most serious consideration and that has been and remains crucial in many different religious universes.

One can draw from numerous religious worlds to illustrate this link between sacred rites and the harmony and functioning of nature, a link that is the logical consequence of the religious view based on the instrumentality of the Logos in the genesis and ordering of the world of nature on the one hand and revelation from which sacred rites, as divinely ordained institutions, originate on the other. In fact, all the religious traditions . . . provide many illustrations of the principle under discussion, namely the link between sacred rites and the order of nature. . .

Turning to Islam, we see that, according to a saying of the Prophet or *hadith*, God placed the Earth for Muslims as a mosque. That is why a Muslim can pray anywhere in virgin nature as long as it is not ritually defiled, and that is why the space of the mosque, built in urban settings already removed from nature, is an extension of the space of virgin nature. The rite of the daily prayers (*salah*) is therefore closely bound to the Earth, which has been designated by God as the ground upon which the most sacred rite of the religion is performed. As for the times of the prayers, they are astronomically determined and correspond to cosmic moments. The prayers not only rejuvenate the body and soul of man, but also emphasize the harmony of human life with the rhythms of nature and fortify and complement nature's harmony.

It is very significant that the central part of the daily prayers is the recitation of the opening chapter of the Qur'an or *al-Fatihah*, which is comprised of verses whose verb is in the plural rather than the singular form. Men and women stand before God directly on the Earth sanctified specifically for Muslim prayers and utter such verses as "Thee do *we* worship," "In Thee do *we* seek refuge," and "lead *us* unto the Straight Path." They are therefore praying not only for themselves, but for the whole of Creation. On the deepest level in the daily prayers, man prays as the *khalifat Allah* or the vice-regent of God on behalf of not only humanity but the whole of the natural order for which he was placed by God on Earth as vice-regent. There is definitely a dimension of the prayers involving the natural ambience around man and which one "feels" concretely upon performing the prayers.

The same cosmic rapport is to be seen in the rite of the pilgrimage or *hajj* to Makkah [Mecca], the center of the Islamic world, the city that is also the earthly intersection of the *axis mundi* [center of the earth], and those circumambulating around the Kaaba emulate the circumambulation of the angels around the Divine Throne (*al-'arsh*). There is definitely a cosmic dimension to this rite, which has been elaborated in many traditional sources. Furthermore, the rapport between sacred rites and the harmony and order of nature is so much emphasized in Islam that, according to a *hadith* [an instructive story about/from Muhammed], the world will not come to an end as long as there are people on Earth who remember the name of God and continue to invoke "Allah, Allah," a practice central to the rituals of Sufism [Islamic mysticism]. In Islamic esoteric teachings, there are also elaborations concerning the spiritual hierarchy that sustains the visible Universe and the power of *walayah*, usually translated as "sanctity" in Sufism, which governs the world invisibly, a power without which the order of nature would turn into chaos and the world would flounder. Even on the popular level, throughout the Islamic world is the belief that God places on the Earth at all times saintly men who through their presence and the rituals and prayers that they perform preserve the order of nature, and that the rites of Islam, which such beings perform at the highest level, and with the greatest perfection, are necessary not only to uphold social order, but also to enable human beings to live in harmony with nature and to preserve the harmony of nature itself.

According to the text of the Qur'an, all creatures in fact share in man's prayers and praise God, for it states, "The seven Heavens and Earth and all beings therein celebrate His praise, and there is not a thing but sings His praise" (XVII:44). This means that man's prayers, celebration of God's praise and other ritual practices, whose final goal is the remembrance of God, form parts of the chorus of the praise of God by the whole of Creation and a melody in the harmony of "voices" celebrating the Divine, a celebration which on the deepest level is the very substance of all beings. The saint hears the invocation of nature wherever he turns. As the Turkish Sufi poet Yunus Emre sings in one of the most famous poems of the Turkish language about the paradisal reality which virgin nature still reflects and manifests,

> The rivers all in Paradise
> Flow with the word Allah, Allah,
> And ev'ry longing nightingale
> He sings and sings Allah, Allah.

Rites and rituals performed by human beings, therefore, fulfill part of the rites of the whole of Creation, and the refusal of human beings to perform rites destroys the harmony of the natural order. Moreover, to destroy nature and cause the extinction of plants and animals as a result of human ignorance is to murder God's worshippers and silence the voice of the prayer of creatures to the Divine Throne. It is to seek to negate the purpose for which the world of nature was created, for, according to a famous *hadith*, God created the world so that He would be known, and the prayers of natural creatures are none other than their knowing God. It means ultimately that, to destroy nature, is to destroy both the humanity committing such a sin and the natural ambience of such a humanity.

In the religious view of nature in general, there is an economy of the cosmic as well as human orders comprising the spiritual, psychic, and physical realms. Rituals are part and parcel of this economy, making possible the flow of grace, the re-establishment of correspondences, and the revival of pre-established harmonies. Human rites play a central role in the preserving of this harmony on the terrestrial realm where men occupy a central position without being allowed to usurp the right of absoluteness, which belongs to God or the Absolute alone. When human beings refuse to perform sacred rites, a central element of the terrestrial harmony is destroyed and human beings become "worthless" and "useless" as far as the ultimate purpose of Creation is concerned, which is to bear witness to God, to love Him, and ultimately to know Him.

The traditional respect for the human state "so difficult to attain," as the Buddhists assert, and the encouragement to have a family and bring new human beings into the world, as emphasized by other faiths such as Judaism and Islam, are both based on the central thesis that, through the human state, the ultimate purpose of Creation, in which Creation itself plays a central role, can be attained. And this ultimate purpose is itself made possible through the following of religious laws and injunctions, at the heart of which is ritual. That is why in the Islamic world there is a folk saying that the virtue of having a child is to add another person to the world who asserts "There is no divinity but God" (*La ilaha illa'Llah*) and that the value of human life is precisely in being able to fulfill this end for which man was created. To rebel against this purpose is not only to become "useless" from the religious point of view, but also to become a negative agent of destruction running havoc upon the Earth and corrupting it, as the Qur'an asserts.

In Islamic terms, once man refuses to follow the *Shari'ah* [Islamic law] and perform the rites promulgated by it, he can no longer fulfill his function as God's vice-regent on Earth. Rather, he begins to usurp the role of the Divinity for himself. The pertinence of this doctrine to the current environmental crisis is too obvious to require elaboration. Moreover, such a view possesses a profound truth no matter how much a secularized world finds the performance of sacred rites to be irrelevant to the processes and activities of the order of nature and the cosmic ambience within the framework of a worldview that has severed all ties between moral laws and cosmic laws. In fact, it can be asserted that the significance of religion is not only to discipline the passions and provide the lance for St. George to slay the dragon of selfishness, greed, and callousness within the soul—which provides the psychic energy for much of the destruction of the environment—but also to provide rites that, in addition to saving the soul of the individual, play a vital role in the preservation of the invisible harmony of the order of nature and the economy of the cosmos . . . .

To Behold the Sacred Quality of Nature: Concluding Comments

The Earth is bleeding and the natural environment suffering in an unprecedented manner from the onslaught of man. The problem is now too evident to deny, and the solutions proposed are many, but for the most part insufficient. Earth will not be healed by some kind of social engineering or changes in a technology that cannot but treat the world as pure quantity to be manipulated for human needs whether they be real or imaginary. All such actions are no more than cosmetics with an effect that is of necessity only skin deep.

What is needed is a rediscovery of nature as sacred reality and the rebirth of man as the guardian of the sacred, which implies the death of the image of man and nature that has given birth to modernism and its subsequent developments. It does not mean "the invention of a new man" as some have claimed, but rather the resurfacing of the true man, the pontifical man whose reality we still bear within ourselves. Nor does it mean the invention of a sacred view of nature, as if man could ever invent the sacred, but rather the reformulation of the traditional cosmologies and views of nature held by various religions throughout history. It means most of all taking seriously the religious understanding of the order of nature as knowledge corresponding to a vital aspect of cosmic reality and not only subjective conjectures or historical constructs. There must be a radical restructuring of the intellectual landscape to enable us to take this type of knowledge of nature seriously, which means to accept the findings of modern science only within the confines of the limitations that its philosophical suppositions, epistemologies [theories of knowledge], and historical development have imposed upon it, while rejecting completely its totalitarian claims as *the* science of the natural order. It means to rediscover a science of nature that deals with the *existence* of natural objects in their relation to Being, with their subtle as well as gross aspects, with their interrelatedness to the rest of the cosmos and to us, with their symbolic significance and with their nexus [connection or link] to higher levels of existence leading to the Divine Origin of things.

Furthermore, in speaking of the religious view of the order of nature, we must now do so in a global context reflecting the global character of the problem at hand. It is necessary to delve into religions as different as the Shamanic and Hindu, Buddhist and Abrahamic, without a relativization that would destroy the sense of the sacred in each tradition. There are perspectives and schools within most religions that have not paid much attention to the domain of nature, as seen especially in Western Christianity, but within every integral tradition there *are* those schools that have dealt with the domain of nature both in its spiritual and cosmic reality. It is those schools that must be sought and studied across religious frontiers in a manner so as to preserve the authenticity of each tradition while bringing out the spiritual significance of nature in a universal fashion . . . .

On a more practical level, it is necessary to create respect on behalf of the followers of a particular religion for what is held to be sacred in another religion not only in the domain, say, of sacred art and architecture, but also in the world of nature. A Muslim in Benares [a city in India] does not consider the Ganges [River] to be sacred for himself, but must accept its sacredness for the Hindus and respect it, as was done for Hindu holy places by traditional Muslims of Benares for centuries and vice-versa as far as Muslim holy places were concerned; this mutual respect has continued for the most part and still survives to some extent despite [regrettable] communal tragedies. The respect accorded to man-made sites possessing religious significance must also be extended to natural ones despite difficulties that come about when two or three religions claim the same site or land as holy, as we find in Palestine and Israel, or when the economic considerations of a more powerful people confront the belief system of others who consider a particular forest, river, or mountain to be sacred. The despicable record of the modern world in overlooking the claims of others to the sacred not only in an abstract manner but also concretely . . . has been itself a major cause of the present environmental crisis and cannot any longer act as model for future dealings among peoples. In evoking the religious understanding of the order of nature, this sense of respect for the religious teachings concerning nature of religions other than our own must be strengthened in the same way that respect for other human beings or houses of worship of other faiths is encouraged, at least by the majority of those concerned with religion and spirituality on a global scale today.

Religions serve as the source of both an ethics involving the environment and a knowledge of the order of nature. They can abet and strengthen one another in both domains if authentic religious teachings are not compromised and diluted in the face of secularism. This is particularly true of Western Christianity, which for so long has tried to identify itself with a civilization that has grown more secular every day. Traditional Christian teachings even in the domain of nature are in fact much closer to those of other religions than to the modern secularist philosophies of the West . . . .

A study of the religious understanding of nature across religious frontiers also affords the possibility of religions enriching each other or certain religions recollecting aspects of their own heritage (now forgotten) through contact with a living tradition. This is certainly as true for sacred sciences and cosmologies as it is for metaphysics, which survive as central realities in certain traditions in contrast to Christianity where they have been for the most part marginalized or forgotten. Conversely, Christianity and to some extent Western Judaism provide valuable knowledge for non-Western religions concerning the confrontation of religion with secularism and the real nature of modern ideas and modes of thought.

Thus, at this moment in human history, the revival of a sacred view of nature, which can only issue from authentic religion, requires a drawing together of various religions in providing a religious response on both the ethical and intellectual level. It means not only the formulation of a religious ethics toward nature, which would be comprehensible and compelling for the vast majority of the inhabitants of the globe who still live in a religious universe. It also means the formulation of the knowledge of the order of nature and ultimately sacred sciences that can shine like jewels in the light of each particular religious cosmos, which, possessing a light of a color specifically its own, causes the jewels also to glitter in a particular manner unique to its conditions.

Finally, every being in the world of nature not only issues from the Divine Principle or the One, but also reflects Its Wisdom and, to use theistic language, sings the praises of the Lord. The religious understanding of the order of nature, which we can share only on the condition of conforming ourselves to the world of the Spirit, enables us to read the signatures of God upon the face of things and hear their prayers. It thereby re-creates a link between us and the world of nature that involves not only our bodies and psyches, but also the Spirit within us and our final end. It enables us to see the sacred in nature and therefore to treat it not only with respect, but also as part of our greater self. It reminds us how precious is each being created by God and how great a sin to destroy wantonly any creature that by virtue of its existence bears the imprint of the Divine and is witness to the One who is our Origin and End, for as the Arab poet has said,

> In all things there exists a sign from Him:
> Which bears proof that He is One.

wa'Llahu a'lam

Introduction to Letter attributed to Chief Seattle

The Letter attributed to Chief Seattle has a varied and rich tradition. According to popular account, when the American government wanted to purchase land in 1854 in the State of Washington—land that was owned by the Puget Sound Indians in the Pacific Northwest—President Franklin Pierce made known to their chief, Seattle, the government's offer. It is said that Chief Seattle then responded with this letter, a reply that has been described as "the most beautiful and profound statement on the environment ever made."

However, a number of facts must be taken into consideration: First, there are several versions of the "letter" which reflect additions and editing. Second, the original exchange occurred in a speech given by Chief Seattle, not a letter. Third, he did not speak English, and his original words were not recorded.

Further, in 1971, scriptwriter Ted Perry put words into the mouth of Chief Seattle for the movie, "Home." For example, a Northwest Indian would not likely have referred to "rotting buffaloes on the prairie . . . shot from a passing train," because he would not have seen buffalo, the prairie, nor a "smoking iron horse"!

Be that as it may, it *is* correct that the letter attributed to Chief Seattle picks up on a great number of themes and insights that are present in the stories in oral traditions of Native peoples and in literature written about them.

Letter Attributed to Chief Seattle

How can you buy or sell the sky, the warmth of the land? The idea is strange to us. If we do not own the freshness of the air and the sparkle of the water, how can you buy them?

Every part of this earth is sacred to my people. Every shining pine needle, every sandy shore, every mist in the dark woods, every clearing and humming insect is holy in the memory and experience of my people. The sap which coursed through the trees carries the memories of the red man.

The white man's dead forget the country of their birth when they go to walk among the stars. Our dead never forget this beautiful earth, for it is the mother of the red man. We are part of the earth, and it is a part of us. The perfumed flowers are our sisters; the deer, the horse, the great eagle, these are our brothers. The rocky crests, the juices in the meadows, the body heat of the pony, and man—all belong to the same family.

So when the great white Chief in Washington sends word that he wishes to buy our land, he asks much of us. The great Chief sends word he will reserve us a place so that we can live comfortably to ourselves. He will be our father, and we will be his children. So we will consider your offer to buy our land. But it will not be easy. For this land is sacred to us.

This shining water that moves in the streams and the rivers is not just water but the blood of our ancestors. If we sell you our land, you must remember that it is sacred, and you must teach your children that it is sacred and that each ghostly reflection in the clear water of the lakes tells of events and memories in the life of my people. The water's murmur is the voice of my father's father.

The rivers are our brothers, they quench our thirst. The rivers carry our canoes and feed our children. If we sell you our land, you must remember and teach your children, that the rivers are our brothers, and yours, and you must henceforth give the rivers the kindness you would give any brother.

We know that the white man does not understand our ways. One portion of land is the same to him as the next, for he is a stranger who comes in the night and takes from the land whatever he needs. The earth is not his brother, but his enemy, and when he has conquered it, he moves on. He leaves his fathers' graves, and his children's birthright is forgotten. He treats his mother, the earth, and his brother, the sky, as things to be bought, plundered, sold like sheep or bright beads. His appetite will devour the earth and leave behind only a desert.

I do not know. Our ways are different from your ways. The sight of your cities pains the eyes of the red man. But perhaps it is because the red man is a savage and does not understand.

There is no quiet place in the white man's cities. No place to hear the unfurling of leaves in spring, or the rustle of an insect's wings. But perhaps it is because I am a savage and do not understand. The clatter only seems to insult the ears. And what is there to life if a man cannot hear the lonely cry of the whippoorwill or the arguments of the frogs around a pond at night? I am a red man and do not understand. The Indian prefers the soft sound of the wind darting over the face of a pond, and the smell of the wind itself, cleansed by rain or scented with the pine cone.

The air is precious to the red man, for all things share the same breath: The beast, the tree, the man, they all share the same breath. The white men, they all share the same breath. The white man does not seem to notice the air he breathes. Like a man dying for many days, he is numb to the stench. But if we sell you our land, you must remember that the air is precious to us, that the air shares its spirit with all the life it supports. The wind that gave our grandfather his first breath also received his last sigh. And if we sell you our land, you must keep it apart and sacred, as a place where even the white man can go to taste the wind that is sweetened by the meadow's flowers.

So we will consider your offer to buy our land. If we decide to accept, I will make one condition. The white man must treat the beasts of this land as his brothers.

I am a savage, and I do not understand any other way. I have seen a thousand rotting buffaloes on the prairie, left by the white man who shot them from a passing train. I am a savage, and I do not understand how the smoking iron horse can be more important than the buffalo that we kill only to stay alive.

What is man without the beasts? If all the beasts were gone, man would die from a great loneliness of spirit. For whatever happens to the beasts soon happens to man. All things are connected.

You must teach your children that the ground beneath their feet is the ashes of our grandfathers. So that they will respect the land, tell your children that the earth is rich with the lives of our kin. Teach your children what we have taught our children, that the earth is our mother. Whatever befalls the earth befalls the sons of the earth. Man did not weave the web of life, he is merely a strand in it. Whatever he does to the web, he does to himself.

Even the white man, whose God walks and talks with him as friend to friend, cannot be exempt from the common destiny. We may be brothers after all. We shall see. One thing we know, which the white man may one day discover—our God is the same God. You may think now that you own Him as you wish to own our land: But you cannot. He is the God of man, and His compassion is equal for the red man and the white. This earth is precious to Him, and to harm the earth is to heap contempt upon its Creator.

The whites, too, shall pass; perhaps sooner than all other tribes. Contaminate your bed, and you will one night suffocate in your own waste.

But in your perishing, you will shine brightly, fired by the strength of the God who brought you to this land and for some special purpose gave you dominion over this land and over the red man. That destiny is a mystery to us, for we do not understand when the buffalo are all slaughtered, the wild horses are tamed, the secret corners of the forest are heavy with the scent of many men, and the view of the ripe hills are blotted out by talking wires.

Where is the thicket? Gone. Where is the eagle? Gone.

Introduction to article by David Kinsley

There is an inherent difficulty in discussing North American indigenous religion. First, there are hundreds of tribes, and claiming that there is a clear and basic uniformity among them is to unfairly gloss over differences and to presumptuously squeeze them into a collective box. In addition, the stories that largely make-up the content of Native American traditions were preserved and circulated in oral form. That led to the adaptation of stories to local situations and issues, and therefore their fluidity.

Despite these legitimate concerns, David Kinsley is able to negotiate several key themes which seem prominent in the majority of Native American traditions. First, hunting occurred in the context of a respect for animals; hence, hunting was fittingly regarded and undertaken as a "sacred occupation." Indeed, animals "gift" their lives for the survival of the human community. As fellow subjects ("spiritual beings"), animals were not so much pursued as prey, but rather propitiated as fellow members of religious rituals.

Second, cultivating a rapport with animals is "a complementary theme to that of hunting as a sacred occupation." The vision quest was a necessary component of this rapport, enhancing the dependence of the hunter on the very animals he hunted.

Third, this theme of rapport with animals extended to every aspect of the natural world—i.e., a rapport with the land. For example, plants, and especially trees, were regarded as worthy of respect, as possessed of spirit, and as "sources of learning and wisdom."

These three themes point to the Native American foundational perspective that "life was lived in relationship to an environment that was infused with sacrality."

Native American Religion

David Kinsley

Hunting as a Sacred Occupation

There is an abundance of evidence to show that in traditional hunting cultures the hunting of game animals takes place within the context of respect for animals and that hunting itself is understood to be a sacred occupation. A large number of rituals and rules concerning the treatment of animals attest to the fact that in many hunting cultures hunting is as much a religious pursuit as an economic one.

Among the Navaho, who live in the Southwest United States, hunting songs are often sung in the sweat lodge prior to the hunt. These songs recount events in the past in which the world came to be and the spirits of the game animals came to be followed during the hunt to show respect for the animals being hunted. During the hunt itself, the hunters communicate with each other only in gestures in special mime language. Upon returning, the hunter reenters the sweat lodge and undergoes purification. He is not allowed to sleep with his wife until he has undergone this process. As one scholar of the Navaho hunting tradition has put it: "Hunting is altogether a sacred rite."

Among the Kwakiutl of British Columbia, as among many other hunting peoples, hunting is understood to involve a spiritual encounter between the hunter and his prey. Hunting therefore involves considerable ritual; indeed, the entire hunt might be understood as a ritual in which the human hunter propitiates, reveres, and addresses the prey. At the heart of this practice of hunting as a holy occupation is the idea that animals, like humans beings, are conscious social, powerful spiritual beings who must be approached in respectful ways. To a great extent, the hunt is understood to be a ritual, or a part of a ritual, in which the hunter fulfills certain obligations to the game animals so that they can fulfill their role in granting the hunter their meat and fur. Speaking of the Kwakiutl, one writer says:

> The encounter between the . . . hunter and his prey seems to involve a vital interchange. The animal yields its life for the welfare of the hunter and his community. The hunter dedicates himself in turn to the rituals of maintaining the continuity of the life cycle for all. In many instances the hunter submits to ritual preparations for the hunt not, as it is often thought, to insure his success, but as the correct and courteous way of meeting the animal who is going to make him a gift of its life.

The buffalo hunt among the Plains Indians was a grand religious ceremony from beginning to end. The hunt "was preceded by offerings, fasting, prayers, the building of altars, and the smoking of pipes; and the hunt itself was often conducted as the most awesome of ceremonies, begun with panoplied processions and surrounded by ritual prohibitions." Throughout the hunt an attitude of respect and apology was encouraged. "It was considered especially dangerous to laugh or use bad language when hunting. The first animal seen of the chosen species was usually let go, with a speech telling it of the need of the hunter and his people, and asking it to tell the others of its 'tribe' to come and offer themselves to be killed." Shamans accompanied the hunters and were seen as central in attracting the animals to the hunters. The hunters also exerted their spiritual powers in such a way that the animals, who were also considered spiritual beings, were persuaded to give themselves up. The hunt, then, was understood not so much as a chase, in which hunters pursued a frightened and unwilling prey, but as a religious ceremony in which the game animals were propitiated and approached in such a way that they would submit to the will of the hunters, who possessed a superior "medicine."

A very widespread practice among North American hunting peoples was a prayer addressed to the animal that had been killed. Typical of such a prayer, in which the hunter apologized to the dead animal and explained his need, was this Papago hunting prayer to a slain deer: "I kill you because I need food. Do not be angry."

Before and after the hunt, purification rituals and a wide range of taboos or restrictions typically were observed. In many cases, images representing the game animals were prepared and propitiated or revered with elaborate rites in which the animal, or its guardian or representative, was asked to give itself to the hunters. In many cultures, women were forbidden to take part in hunting and were strictly avoided by the male hunters prior to and during the hunt itself. Sexual taboos were enforced, and hunting often involved celibacy on the part of the hunters.

The remains of animals were also the subject of many taboos, rituals, and beliefs, all of which tended to enforce the theme of respect and reverence for the slain animal, which continued to be treated as sacred in some sense. Many of these practices emphasized the theme of not killing any more animals than was necessary for survival and the importance of utilizing all of the animals' parts.

Complementing the theme of the hunt as a ritual or ceremony is the idea among some hunting peoples that animals also perform rituals. A common belief among hunting peoples is that game animals live in societies that are similar to human societies. In the case of large migrations, hunting people sometimes understood these as pilgrimages on which the animals set out to make themselves available to their human counterparts.

The salmon were believed to be a numerous host of spirit beings who had their village out under the western ocean. Those Indians who visited them in visions saw them living in great houses like human beings. Their annual pilgrimages to the mountain streams were seen as a voluntary sacrifice for the benefit of their human friends. Though they seemed to die, the spirits had simply removed their outer "salmon robes," and journeyed back to their undersea homes. But they would return again only if their gifts of flesh were treated with careful respect.

Another common aspect of hunting among traditional North American hunting cultures concerned what we might call conservation. Restraint was exercised in the numbers of any one species killed, the young were often spared so that they could reproduce, and certain species were not hunted during the mating season.

The hunter's weapons were also treated as special. They were much more than utilitarian artifacts used to kill animals. Weapons contained powerful spirits and were often decorated to enhance their spiritual powers. They were highly personal and were frequently buried with a hunter. In short, the hunter's weapons were treated as ritual implements.

Rapport with Animals

Among many North American hunting cultures, cultivating a rapport with animals is a related and complementary theme to that of hunting as a sacred occupation. Young people are taught myths and legends about the past that are central in acquiring their human identity. In many cases, these myths tell of a time when humans and animals were one, when both humans and animals could transform themselves into each other's forms. An implicit theme in these types of tales is the emphasis upon the essential relatedness that exists between human beings and the animals they hunt and subsist upon. These tales suggest that in some mysterious way human beings and animals are very closely and deeply related and that it is their destiny to live out their lives in mutually dependent fashion.

Rapport with animals among hunting peoples in North America also is clearly evident in the vision quest, which usually took place as part of puberty initiation rites. In many tribes, full adulthood was understood to involve the acquisition of a guardian spirit, which was usually accomplished by means of a vision quest. Until and unless a youth acquired a guardian spirit, almost always an animal spirit, that person was not considered a full human being. The vision quest usually involved a rather arduous, lone journey into the wilderness, or to a sacred place, at which the initiate would fast, remain naked and wakeful, and "cry for a vision." The quest would often last several days and usually resulted in the youth's being blessed with a vision, or insight, involving an animal spirit or guardian. That is, the aim of the quest was to make contact with, or establish rapport with, the world of animals, to experience directly the powers latent in the animal world.

This vision, or this contact or rapport, marked an expansion of vision or understanding outside the human realm into the animal realm. It extended one's identity to the animal world; it completed one's identity, as it were. The vision quest and the gaining of a guardian spirit meant that the youth searched deeply into the secrets and powers of the animal world, gained insight into that realm, and as a result of such insight acquired special powers of discernment that enabled him or her, but particularly males, to function more effectively in the world as a hunter. As a result of the vision quest, the youth usually became linked with an animal spirit in a lifelong alliance in which the youth was empowered and the spirit and members of the spirit's species were revered by the youth. In more religious or theological language, the Indian youth sought a revelation from the animal realm, a revelation that would mature and empower him or her. Among many North American hunting cultures, then, a mature human being was a person who had been blessed and empowered by an animal spirit, who had established rapport with the animal world, and who had insight into its essential nature.

In short, a mature hunter was one who understood deeply the nature of animals and who felt dependent upon them for his own essential being and discernment. In this sense, the hunter's economic dependence on animals was matched by his deep regard and respect for them as spiritual guardians and teachers. The hunter also typically received from the guardian spirit special "medicine" songs or chants that enabled him to be effective in the hunt. The vision quest, then, enhanced the hunter's relationship to, understanding of, and dependence upon the very animals he hunted. This enhanced rapport strengthened the emphasis in the culture generally upon revering and respecting the animals that were the very basis of survival. It strengthened what we might refer to as the youth's ecological spirituality or sensitivity.

Rapport with the Land

In many native North American Indian religions, the theme of rapport with animals is extended to every aspect of the "natural" world—to plants, rivers, rocks, and mountains. In many cases, spiritual kinship with the land is fostered and nurtured and gives rise to what we might call an ecologically sensitive outlook on the world. Black Elk, a Sioux holy man who lived in the late nineteenth century, addressed this short prayer to Mother Earth: "Every step that we take upon you should be done in a sacred manner; each step should be as a prayer."

An important theme is often the interrelatedness of human beings with all aspects of the natural world, the embeddedness of human beings in the natural world. In some cases this theme is expressed in terms of emphasizing that one underlying or overarching spirit or essence pervades all things. In the words of a Hopi Indian: "The whole universe is enhanced with the same breath—rocks, trees, grass, earth, all animals, and men." Or as a Taos Pueblo Indian put it: "We are in one nest." Black Elk, again, expressed the theme of relatedness this way: "With all beings and all things we shall be as relatives."

Just as animals were understood to be spiritual beings toward whom human beings should show respect, so too were plants considered worthy of respect and possessed of spirit. Trees, in particular, were often revered as sources of learning and wisdom. Walking Buffalo, an Indian of the Stoney tribe of Canada, said this about trees:

> Did you know that trees talk? Well they do. They talk to each other, and they'll talk to you if you listen. Trouble is, white people don't listen. They never learned to listen to the Indians so I don't suppose they'll listen to other voices in nature. But I have learned a lot from trees—sometimes about the weather, sometimes about animals, sometimes about the Great Spirit.

In the following remarks of the Sioux chief Sitting Bull, the oak tree is appreciated for what it can teach human beings about themselves and the world:

> I wish all to know that I do not propose to sell any part of my country, nor will I have whites cutting our timber along the rivers, especially the oak. I am particularly fond of the little groves of oak trees. I love to look at them, because they endure wintry storm and the summer's heat, and—not unlike ourselves—seem to flourish by them.

Gathering plants for medicine was routinely undertaken as a sacred enterprise accompanied with rituals and songs. Similarly, plants gathered for food were treated with respect, and only as much as was needed was gathered. As in hunting, plants were often directly addressed before being gathered or harvested. An apology was made to the plant explaining the human being's need, and often also an offering was made to the plant. In some cases, for example among the Apaches, many plants were called "brothers" and "sisters."

The ceremonial and ritual aspects of agriculture among many North American Indians were central. In many cases, agriculture was understood to be a holy occupation. Peter Price, a Navajo, said this about growing crops: "Even before you start to plant, you sing songs. You continue this during the whole time your crops are growing. You cannot help but feel that you are in a holy place when you go through your fields and they are doing well." Individual plants were treated as holy beings among the Hopi and Navaho and were tended and nursed with the care one gives an infant. The whole process of growing corn was pervaded by rituals and holy tradition.

> The ripe maize was treated with the greatest respect, called 'mother' and associated closely with Mother Earth. No metal knives were allowed to touch the cornstalks by some tribes, nor were any kernels left scattered on the ground. The harvested corn was stored carefully in underground cache pits that had been blessed ritually. Seed corn was consecrated and strictly protected.

In short, corn was considered sacred and every aspect of its cultivation among certain tribes had ritual or religious overtones. Every stage of maize cultivation had an appropriate song among the Indians of the Southwest United States, and growing corn was described as "singing up the corn." "Ears of maize were powerful talismans. Among the Zunis, the newborn infant was presented with an ear of maize, receiving a 'corn name.' An ear of maize was put into the place of death as the 'heart of the deceased' and later used as seed corn. 'Corn is the same as a human being, only it is holier', said a Navajo."

Native Indian rapport with the natural world was also evident in their reverence for the landscape in which they lived. For many groups of Indians, the land was textured with sacred places and traditions. As in the case of the Australian Aborigines, the land was often alive with sacred power and meaning for Native American Indians. N. Scott Momaday, an Indian writer from the United States, says:

> From the time the Indian first set foot upon this continent, he has centered his life in the natural world. He is deeply invested in the earth, committed to it both in his consciousness and in his instinct. To him the sense of place is paramount. Only in reference to the earth can he persist in his true identity.

For many native groups, the land was understood to be inhabited by powerful spirits. To know the land, and the places that were inhabited by spirits, was very much a part of becoming an adult, a mature person. "Part of the process of initiating youths into the tribe involved teaching them the names of hundreds of sacred localities." The land was also understood to be inhabited by the spirits of the ancestors and was sacred for that reason too. The land was understood to be invested with the history and culture of the tribes that lived upon it.

Among some tribes in North America, the earth itself was treated as a powerful being toward whom great respect was appropriate.

During the spring, when plants are starting to grow, the Pueblo Indians believe the earth is tender and treat her with special care. Often they remove heels from their shoes and the shoes from their horses' hooves during that season. [An anthropologist] reports that he once asked a Hopi: "Do you mean to say, then, that if I kick the ground with my foot, it will botch everything up, so nothing will grow?" He said, "Well I don't know whether that would happen or not, but it would just really show what kind of person you are."

The Indian prophet Smohalla of the United States Northwest, when asked by the United States government to settle his people on a reservation and take up agriculture and mining, replied:

You ask me to plow the ground! Shall I take a knife and tear my mother's bosom? Then when I die she will not take me to her bosom to rest. You ask me to dig for stone! Shall I dig under her skin for her bones? Then when I die I cannot enter her body to be born again. You ask me to cut grass and make hay and sell it, and be rich like the white men! But how dare I cut off my mother's hair?

Among many North American Indian tribes, then, life was lived in relationship to an environment that was infused with sacrality. Animals, plants, rocks, trees, and the earth itself were understood to possess spiritual power. To relate intensely to these powers was the aim of much native Indian religion. To be cut off from that power, to live in isolation from it, to be unaware or ignorant of that power, was to live, in some sense, an incomplete, immature, stifled existence. To relate to that power, to gain an intense rapport or relationship with it, was to harness great energy and discernment, to become fully human. It was to flow with the natural rhythms of the world and by so flowing to acquire a sense of beauty and capability. This feeling of completeness, power, and beauty is captured well, I think, in this short Innuit poem:

> The great sea
> has set me adrift
> it moves me
> as a weed in a great river
> earth and the great weather
> move me
> have carried me away
> and move my inward parts with joy.

Introduction to article by Joel Martin

Joel Martin points out in this article that spirituality affected everything that Native Americans did, from cooking to dressing to marrying to cutting hair. "Our land, our religion, and our life are one." Wisdom came "by paying attention to the natural world."

He illustrates this by examining first, the Hopis of the Southwest, and the centrality of growing corn in their culture; then the Koyukons of Alaska, and the centrality of hunting animals in their culture; and last, the White Mountain Apaches of Arizona and the centrality of their sacred stories linking ethics to the landscape.

A striking observation that he makes is that Native American religion is tied not just to a way of life, but also to a particular landscape. Because of this, the religion is not portable; it may not be exported. This distinguishes Native American religion from world religions such as Christianity, Buddhism, and Islam, which are evangelistic religions and can be practiced anywhere.

From a Native American perspective, the land even goes so far as to aid and teach the moral life. Stories related to the land—a particular site or spot—are used to prohibit some behaviors and sanction others. "The land looks after us," as a contemporary Apache man concludes.

The goal of the Native American, then, was to live a good life in a sacred landscape. A moral person was one who lived attuned to the rhythms of nature.

The Land Looks After Us

Joel Martin

Circling Earth

For some American Indians involved in Native American religions, life un-folds as a rich drama. This drama plays out in a world filled with spiritual forces and shaped by them. Everything can mean something. Little is separate from religious influence. Spiritually attuned Native American men and women seek multiple ways to express their religious visions. Their spirituality can affect how they cook, eat, dance, paint, tell stories, mold pottery, dye clothes, decorate their bodies, design their homes, organize their villages, court lovers, marry, bury, dress, speak, make love, cut their hair, and so on. Wisdom comes by paying at-tention to the living world, discerning the spiritual dimension within it, and de-bating its significance with others in a community. For people holding this per-spective, everyday realities can carry extraordinary significance. Dreams may matter. Mountains can harbor gods. Even practical activities can carry religious meaning. Agriculture can be sacred; hunting holy.

Some Hopis view the world this way. Gifted farmers, they grow corn in the near-desert of northeastern Arizona. For some Hopis, planting and raising corn possesses a spiritual significance. In contemplating it, they like to refer to one of their creation stories. These stories depict the origins of important realities, prac-tices, and institutions. Some tell how land came to be. Others account for the origins of agriculture, medicines, animal behaviors, the movements of the sun and moon, the song of birds, the causes of sickness, the foundations of cultural traditions, the names of specific landmarks, and so on. Many Native American creation stories say that the original people emerged from the interior of the earth. The earth, in this type of account, resembles a mother. In her womb, she nurtures the proto-humans. When they are ready, they emerge to the surface to become complete human beings. According to the Hopis' emergence story, before their ancestors left the underworld they were asked to choose how they would live. They elected a hard and humble life raising blue corn. Later, the god Masaw taught the Hopis the right way to plant and care for his crop.

Not all Hopis nurture relationships with Masaw and other Hopi gods, nor do all plant blue corn. Like any other people, Hopis disagree among themselves regarding religious life. They struggle with the challenges of making sense of reality. They work hard to reconcile religious traditions with the post-modern world of computers, corporations, and capitalism. Sometimes they fail, grow frustrated, argue, and divide. Nevertheless, an impressive truth remains: For fifteen hundred years Hopi people have planted blue corn in the same place. It is likely they will continue to do so for many more generations. One of their mesa-top villages, Old Oraibi, contends for the title of the oldest continuously inhabited village in North America. What their ceremonial chiefs and elders declared in 1951 remains true today for many Hopis: "Our land, our religion, and our life are one."

That identical statement could be affirmed by many of the Koyukon people of Alaska, but they would give it different content. Living far to the north where agriculture is impossible, they nevertheless connect their religion with the landscape and their way of life. For them, however, the sacred dimension of life is not explored through digging dirt and planting seeds, but through observing and hunting the animals of central Alaska. Many Koyukon people affirm that animals have spirits. Some of these spirits—living in the brown bear, black bear, wolverine, lynx, wolf, and otter, among other animals—are very powerful.

An elaborate moral code governs how the Koyukon relate to these spirits. The code, in turn, derives from oral tradition, a rich collection of stories set in the Distant Time, the time of beginnings. These stories teach the Koyukon what and who is sacred. Animals figure a large role in these stories, exercising a powerful influence on creation itself. For example, a story recorded by anthropologist Richard Nelson recalls the influence Raven had on rivers. Kk'adonts'idnee, "in the Distant Time it is said," Raven made the rivers so that they flowed both ways, "upstream on one side and downstream on the other. But this made life too easy for humans, he decided, because their boats could drift along in either direction without paddling. So Raven altered his creation and made the rivers flow only one way, which is how they remain today."

Guided by Distant Time stories, the Koyukon people enjoy an intimacy with their surroundings that is difficult for outsiders to comprehend. To be sure, outsiders can learn some of the Koyukon people's stories. They can begin to appreciate the moral code by which the Koyukon live. But without actually living as Koyukons live and living where they live, outsiders can never fully understand their religion or convert to it. Koyukon religion, like that of the Hopis, is tied to a way of life, a distinct community, a particular language, and a specific landscape. The link to land distinguishes Koyukon religion from "world religions" such as Christianity, Buddhism, and Islam. Those religions are different, portable; they can be practiced anywhere. Koyukon religion, in contrast, cannot be exported from central Alaska. It belongs there just as surely as Hopi religion belongs in northern Arizona. Koyukon missionaries will never knock on your door. Traditional Hopis will not try to convert you.

Nor will traditional White Mountain Apaches. Like the religions of traditional Hopis and Koyukons, their religion is land-based. It ties White Mountain Apaches to a specific landscape in a profound way. Traditional White Mountain Apaches not only revere the land, they look to it for guidance. Their sacred stories link ethics to the landscape. For White Mountain Apaches, religion means nothing without dirt; morality comes from the earth.

White Mountain Apaches associate thousands of specific sites in east central Arizona with specific traditional stories. These stories relate the powerful actions of gods, the comic antics of cultural heroes like Old Man Owl, the noble struggles of their human ancestors, even the everyday triumphs and failures or contemporary Apache men and women. By telling these stories, Apaches invoke the memory of what took place at specific places. By selecting carefully which stories to tell at a particular instance, Apaches communicate important moral lessons to each other. In doing so, they can teach each other how to lead a good life, a life untainted by jealousy, envy, or arrogance. Among Apaches who know the language, the stories, and the landscape, an amazingly condensed form of communication becomes possible. By merely mentioning a strategically selected place-name, a thoughtful Apache can invoke the right story to communicate a spiritual truth of life-changing power to another Apache. This takes intellectual quickness, knowledge of the storytelling tradition, a good memory, and the courage to take a risk. Apache religion depends upon individual initiative and communal involvement.

For example, one summer . . . an Apache worried about her younger brother's inattention to Apache religion. He had handled snakeskin, a careless act sure to produce spiritual harm. A friend told her, "*Tsee Hadigaiye yu agodzaa.*" In English, according to anthropologist Keith Basso, this means, "it happened at Line of White Rocks Extends Up and Out, at this very place!" A place-name, *Tsee Hadigaiye yu agodzaa*, evokes a specific story associated with that site. The story tells of how an innocent youth behaved irresponsibly, suffered, but ultimately recovered and learned the values of patience and mindfulness. By mentioning the right place-name, the woman reminded her friend of an appropriate story. This gave the worried woman a way to understand what was happening. She could connect her brother's error with a treasured story from her people's tradition, a story tied to the sacred landscape around them. It also comforted the woman to know that her friend cared how she was coping, that her friend had labored to remember a story in the first place, and selected a reassuring one in the second.

Another example illustrates the importance of the landscape among contemporary Apaches, the way physical environment, morality, and religion are fused for many of them. A young woman behaved disrespectfully at a girls' puberty ceremony, wearing pink plastic curlers instead of letting her hair flow free. The next day, at a meal that included the girl and several other people, her grandmother told the story about an Apache man who copied white people too much. Later arrested for rustling, the man came to a bad end. By telling the story, the grandmother sought to "shoot" the young woman, to make her reflect on her ways. Among the Apaches, as among many Native American peoples, women possess spiritual power, and respected elder women exercise important spiritual and social authority. The grandmother's story worked. Each time the young woman passed the place where the man had lived, she thought of her own behavior and determined to lead a good life, an Apache life. Her grandmother's story shamed her, now the landscape reminded her. "I know that place," she admitted to a non-Apache friend. "It stalks me every day." To this young Apache women, the landscape speaks a powerful moral message. Nick Thompson, an Apache man, concludes: "The land looks after us. The land keeps badness away." To Apaches, the landscape aids moral development and sustains religious life . . .

Introduction to article by Christopher Key Chapple

In this article, Professor Chapple acknowledges the centrality of *ahimsa*—non-violence or non-injury—in the religious traditions of India, whether Hinduism, Buddhism, or Jainism. He then shares several anecdotes that "show the ongoing concern for not hurting living beings in India" and traces the history of non-violence specifically in Hinduism.

A part of this, perhaps inevitably, leads to the figure of Mohandas K. ("Mahatma"—'Great Soul') Gandhi, who designed and led a movement for Indian "home rule" (independence).

The article ends with a discussion of the contrast between a religion that emphasizes the sacredness of life and respect for all life forms and that does so in a country that promotes industrial growth which has befouled the air, polluted the rivers, and ravaged the land and its resources.

Ecological Nonviolence and the Hindu Tradition

Christopher Key Chapple

Nonviolence has long been central to the religious traditions of India, espe-cially Jainism, Buddhism, and certain schools of Hinduism. From the early pro-nouncement that "all things want to live" (*Acaranga Sutra* 1:1) to Vyasa's defi-nition of nonviolence as the "absence of oppression toward all living beings in all respects and for all times" (*Bhasyaon Yoga Sutra*, 11:31) to the Dalai Lama's assertion that "all beings primarily seek peace, comfort, security; life is as dear to mute creatures as it is to a man," religion in India has consistently upheld the sanctity of life, whether human, animal, or in the case of the Jainas, elemental. The message has provided an unparalleled concern for harmony amongst life forms, leading to a common ethos based on minimal consumption of natural resources, particularly for members of religious orders. In the discussion that follows, we will begin with some anecdotes that show the ongoing concern for not hurting living beings in India. We will then trace the history of nonviolence in India specifically in the Hindu tradition. The village economy proposed by Gandhi will be discussed briefly as a modern application of nonviolent princi-ples. This all will be juxtaposed with some harsh realities from the industrial-ized, modern Indian landscape, followed by possible solutions that traditional religious wisdom may hold for the current and growing ecological dilemma both in India and the world.

A colleague once told me a story wherein a development worker was con-fronted with and confounded by nonviolence in the context of attitudes in Indian regarding the worth of animal life. It seems that several years ago a major factor contributing to food shortages in India was the prevalence of and voraciousness of the rodent population: A significant percentage of each year's grain crop was devoured by rats. An American was called in from a development agency to assess the situation. He immediately proposed poison. Shocked and affronted, his Indian co-worker asserted that such a solution simply would not be acceptable; to kill the rats would be in violation of nonviolence, the primary ethical virtue of the Hindu and Jaina traditions. After much discussion, a variety of alternatives were considered and one proved to be satisfactory for curtailing the rat population in the spirit of ahimsa [nonviolence]. The grain storage facilities were placed on stilts, thus stymying the vermin without directly injuring them.

In another demonstration of resourcefulness in using nonviolent techniques, a woman from India told me a story that occurred during her childhood in West Bengal. An important local temple had become overrun with ants. The offering to the enshrined deity were being consumed, not by the gods or the resident priests, but by swarms and swarms of industrious insects. To kill them was unthinkable, but their presence grew increasingly intolerable. Finally, one enterprising temple-goer proposed a solution which at first seemed preposterous but, due to lack of alternatives, was given a try. Next to the existing temple a new shrine was erected, to and for the ants. Rather than being composed of stone, this religious center was comprised solely of sugar cane, and included offerings of refined sugar. Soon, the human temple was free of pestilence and, judging by the number of devotees, the ant temple soon outstripped its human counterpart in popularity.

Both of these anecdotes demonstrate common-sense methods of avoiding harm to living systems, whether they be insect, mammal or the earth itself. From the earliest period of historical Jainism and Buddhism, and from the post-Vedic Hinduism onward, there has been a persistent concern in the history of Indian civilization for protecting life. The practice of nonviolence stems from a world view that challenges Western presuppositions regarding life and has spawned a thorough-going respect for humans, animals, plants, and even elements.

In order to understand why this practice has become tantamount to Indian religious traditions, the meaning of life must be investigated. Why is life sacred? For various ancient thinkers of India, life is seen as eternally existent: Each life state is interrelated and interchangeable. All life is made up of elements and passes from one form into another. The human condition is the highest, most desirable form of life, but is not necessarily a permanent condition. According to the *Chandogya Upanisad* (5:10), the elements of the body, when cremated, enter into the atmosphere, join with the rain, return to the earth, enter into plants, are consumed by humans, and form the seeds for new life. There is a continuity of substance between one's body and a future embodiment.

Various Hindu texts proclaim the sanctity of life and suggest consequent ethical norms. The *Yajur Veda* (36.18) proclaims: "May all beings look at me with a friendly eye, may I do likewise, and may we all look on each other with the eyes of a friend." The *Laws of Manu*, which have played a great role in shaping Hindu society [this is the source of the caste system], list nonviolence among the rules to be performed by all castes, along with truthfulness, non-stealing, purity, and control of senses. In regard to meat-eating, the *Laws of Manu* contain three separate recommendations: That only "kosher" meat may be eaten; that only meat used in ritual may be eaten; and that one should eat no meat:

Vegetarianism, not in evidence among the Rg Vedic peoples, eventually became one of the principal designators of purity, to be strictly adhered to by the Brahmin castes as a demonstration of their commitment to nonviolence.

One should never do that to another which one regards as injurious to one's own self. This, in brief, is the rule of righteousness. Yielding to desire and acting differently, one becomes guilty of nonvirtue.

Mahabharata XVIII:113:8

Those high-souled persons who desire beauty, faultlessness of limbs, long life, understanding, mental and physical strength, and memory should abstain from acts of injury.

Mahabharata XVIII:115:8

Ahimsa [nonviolence; noninjury] is the highest dharma [duty or righteousness]. Ahimsa is the best austerity. Ahimsa is the greatest gift. Ahimsa is the highest self-control. Ahimsa is the highest friend. Ahimsa is the highest truth. Ahimsa is the highest teaching.

Mahabharata XVIII:116:37-41

The purifications of one who does ahimsa are inexhaustible. Such a one is regarded as always performing sacrifices, and is the father and mother of all beings.

Mahabharata XVIII:115:41

In these passages from the *Mahabharata*, nonviolence or *ahimsa* is the best of all actions, giving birth to all righteousness or *dharma* and serving as the best means for purification.

In the classical Yoga system, nonviolence is cited as the basis and the reason for all ethical practices. The commentator, Vyasa, as noted earlier, defines nonviolence as the absence of injuriousness towards all living being in all respects and for all times. It is said to result in the alleviation of enmity in the proximity of one practicing nonviolence (*Yoga sutra* 11:35). It is acknowledged by Vyasa that circumstantial exigencies might preclude the total practice of nonviolence. He gives as examples several cases. The first is that of the fisherman who only injures fish for his own survival. The second is when one vows to abstain from killing only in a special place. Another is when one observes harmlessness exclusively on particular days. In another hypothetical situation, violence could be approved because it is for the gods. . . . Or, like a fisherman, a warrior can justify violence as his profession. In the final analysis, however, the yogi is required to practice nonviolence in its greatest sense, unrestricted by caste, place, time, or circumstance. Nonviolence here is regarded as the foremost spiritual discipline, to be strictly adhered to by aspiring yogis.

The performance of action in light of nonviolence requires, regardless of tradition, that the performer of any activity see the implications of his or her act and also reside in the vision that another person is, in a fundamental sense, not different from oneself. Philosophically, nondifference of self and other provides the basis for performing nonviolence. Within the context of the Indian quest for liberation, nonviolence provides an important step toward the direct perception of the sacredness of all life. It serves to free one from restricted notions of self and opens one to a more full awareness of and sensitivity toward the wants and needs of others, animals, and the world of the elements, all of which exist in reciprocal dependence.

A study of nonviolence in India would not be complete without reference to Mahatma Gandhi, who drew upon existing tradition as learned primarily from Jainas (with input from Tolstoy and British vegetarians) to develop a campaign for national independence. It is not possible to fully explore in the present study Gandhi's theories and applications of nonviolence, much of which pertain to political action. However, one phase of Gandhi's work does hold possible implications for a post-modern approach to the environment: His proposed revitalization of village economies, based on the principles of nonviolence (*ahimsa*) and nonpossession (*aparigraha*). The purpose of Gandhi's campaign was to make villages self-sufficient, able to cooperate without the importation of foreign-produced goods. His means to achieve this was through spinning and weaving cloth and revitalizing other crafts within each village, requiring that schools include these skills as part of the curriculum. Although the aim of this program was to subvert the colonial economic dependence thrust upon India by the British, and despite the fact that Gandhi himself did not object to industrialization, the conservation of energy inherent in the system could be effectively used to counter some of the environmental peril posed in the post-modern world.

Nonviolence, in the classical texts and traditions we have examined, is an ethical practice undertaken to lessen one's bondage and suffering. It necessitated an austere, simple lifestyle. For Mahatma Gandhi, steeped in the Indian climate of nonviolence and prompted into action by social oppression, nonviolence became a rallying point for a social movement. He observed that in order for nonviolence to be put into effect, it must not be limited to oneself. "To me, virtue ceases to have any value if it is cloistered or possible only for individuals" (Gandhi, *My Socialism*, p. 36). For Gandhi . . . the propriety of nonviolence has to be extended into the wider net of one's interrelationships. Gandhi did not separate the practice of nonviolence from economic realities. He wrote:

> I must confess that I do not draw a sharp distinction between economics and ethics. Economics that hurt the moral well-being of an individual or a nation are immoral and, therefore, sinful. . . . True economics . . . stands for social justice, it promotes the good of all equally, including the weakest, and is indispensable for decent life.
>
> *Ibid.*, p. 34

Strictly speaking, no activity and no industry are possible without a certain amount of violence, no matter how little. Even the very process of living is impossible without a certain amount of violence. What we have to do is to minimize it to the greatest extent possible. Indeed, the very word "nonviolence," a negative word, means that it is an effort to abandon the violence that is inevitable in life. Therefore, whoever believes in nonviolence will engage himself in occupations that involve the least possible violence. By minimizing one's needs and the means used to produce those needs, life, according to Gandhi, holds more potential for happiness.

These ideals are not found only in Gandhian analysis. [Economist] E.F. Schumacher has also cited Buddhism as a tradition wherein the process of consumption is informed by higher values:

> It is not wealth that stands in the way of liberation, but the attachment to wealth; not the enjoyment of pleasurable things, but the craving for them. The keynote of Buddhist economics, therefore, is simplicity and nonviolence. From an economist's point of view, the marvel of the Buddhist way of life is the utter rationality of its pattern—amazingly small means leading to extraordinarily satisfactory results.
>
> *Buddhist Economics*, p. 699

Schumacher has elaborated on this theme in *Small is Beautiful*, an eloquent plan for economic reorganization. . . . Schumacher makes a dramatic point that updates the traditional Indian concern for life in light of potential ecological disaster. To use up nonrenewable goods, a possibility unconceivable in classical India, is the ultimate form of violence, one that eventually could destroy all life forms.

> Nonrenewable goods must be used only if they are indispensible, and then only with the greatest care and the most meticulous concern for conservation. To use them heedlessly or extravagantly is an act of violence, and while complete nonviolence may not be attainable on this earth, there is nonetheless a duty on man to aim at the ideal of nonviolence in all he does.
>
> *Ibid.*, p. 699

As never before, humans now possess the ability to use, abuse, and ultimately destroy our own ecosystem.

[Cultural anthropologist] Thomas Berry has noted that much of the erosion of the earth is due to increasingly industrialized technology and expansion of transportation networks. Both of these take natural resources, convert them into "consumables," transport them across continents, and quickly process them into garbage. Gandhi himself prophesized the dire effects of environmental decay:

> This land of ours was once, we are told, the abode of the gods. It is not possible to conceive gods inhabiting a land which is made hideous by the smoke and din of mill chimneys and factories, and whose roadways are traversed by rushing engines, dragging numerous cars crowded with men who know not for the most part what they are after, who are often absent-minded and whose tempers do not improve by being uncomfortably packed like sardines in boxes and finding themselves in the midst of utter strangers who would

oust them if they could and whom they would, in their turn, oust similarly. I refer to these things because they are held to be symbolic of material progress.
But they add not an atom to our happiness.

Gandhi, *My Socialism*, p. 34

The solutions Gandhi proposed to counter the ills of colonialism can also be
put into effect to redress this new and ultimately equally deleterious dilemma.
By producing necessities by hand, more natural products are produced, less energy is consumed in production, and, if the village is fully operative, little or no
transportation of goods is needed. The nonviolent Gandhian life style serves as
an alternative to consumer-based economies, minimizing the consumption of
nonreusable resources.

The Buddha and others in classical India addressed the issue of existential
suffering and its resolution through transcendence or spiritual liberation. This
may seem lofty, removed from, and irrelevant to the grim reality of environmental ravage. The spiritual traditions of India present to us an earth that is living, breathing, an earth whose many creatures are literally to be regarded as our
mother and father. This vision of man's intimate link with the natural world extends throughout much of premodern society; more than most traditions, however, Jainism, Buddhism, and Hinduism have systematically asserted and proven
the pervasiveness and sanctity of life. Nonetheless, it cannot be denied that the
traditional world of Asia is rapidly being eroded by the Amero-European-
spawned technological trance. The colonial era in India and Maoist revolution in
China stalled the process by several decades in each of these countries, but the
21st century will see an unparalleled explosion of "development" similar to that
experienced in Japan and Korea in the second part of the 20th century . . . Unfortunately, in each of these situations, the drive for modernization is taking
place without the benefit of the lessons that have been learned in the now post-
modern Western world.

If I may again resort to anecdote, let me relate an experience I had while in
India that left a profound impression. We have explored a few aspects of India's
long history of regard for human life, and we have seen examples of the great
care which has taken to preserve and protect life in its many forms. However, if
we look at other aspects of Indian civilization, the converse is also true, particularly in regard to contemporary attitudes towards industrialization. During a trip
to Kerala a few years ago, I was stunned by the rampant pollution caused by the
chemical manufacturers. We had spent a couple hours traveling by bus to the
birthplace of Sankaracharya when, all of a sudden, the lush, verdant landscape
gave way to brown stubble and the sweet tropical air became foul with chemical
stench, rivaling the worst of what one encounters in New Jersey or Niagara
Falls. We approached the plant—ironically a producer of fertilizer—and were
"welcomed" by a dour crowd of employees, who seemed none too thrilled with
their factory-dominated existence. As we pulled away from the plant, I com-
mented to one of our hosts that the pollution seemed extreme. He blithely replied that fortunately no one lived nearby. However, as we rounded a bend, a

construction project was underway, well within the umbrella of foul air—new housing for factory workers. As we left the general locale and returned to the world of rice paddies, rickshaws, and coconuts, I could not help but fear for the longterm effects of apparently unregulated industry. A couple of years later, sadly, my sense of foreboding was confirmed: The Union Carbide disaster in Bhopal took the lives of over 2200 persons in Central India.

What can be learned from this land contrasts a country that professes religions of total harmlessness and yet tolerates industrial growth that has rocketed India into the position of number ten in the world. In a sense, we are talking of two Indias—a world, a culture which is among the very oldest on the planet earth, and a country which is entering into industrialization almost two hundred years after the developed world. The former has a great wealth of insight to offer, a legacy of philosophy, religion, and ethical practice that has influenced both American and European thought and, in the form of Buddhism, has influenced virtually all of Asia. The latter is on the threshold of change—a teeming population with the bulk of the people equipped with a world view equivalent to that of 14th century Europe. The poignancy of Bhopal hit home when a man was quoted by the press as exclaiming, "We simply do not understand! Floods and fires we can understand. But no one has ever heard of poisonous gases!"

There is an increasing tendency to export the worst work of industry to the largely unregulated and unsuspecting Third World. As environmental restrictions were tightened and labor costs increased in the North American continent, the business community looked eastward, not for new markets and sources of raw materials as in colonial days, but for less stringent or nonexistent pollution restriction and for a large supply of willing, inexpensive labor. However, whereas the theological and explorative view toward the world gave explicit sanction to the industrialization of America and Europe, threads of Asian culture, evidenced in the classical traditions surveyed above and recently put into action by Mahatma Gandhi, will hopefully cause the psyche of Asia to pause and reassess whether untrammeled industrialization is worth the risks involved. The Bhopal incident could not have occurred out of the context of traditional Asia values; the Indian doctrines of noninterference and nonviolence would have precluded the conscious development of such toxic substances. Furthermore, the contemporary India peasant lacks the framework for coping with such oddities as poison gas. It is still inconceivable that so subtle and sacred an element as the air itself could carry death to thousands.

Much must be learned of our history in the West to comprehend where technology has failed us. And, as the literature on environmental ethics . . . indicates, a solution will only be effective in the Euro-American context if it is reasonable in an Aristotelean sense—well-argued, analytical, and ultimately in keeping with the Western *telos* [purpose; end] of human betterment. The mainstream of such discussion is that the environment must be spared because ultimately man himself is threatened. From Jainism, Buddhism, and Hinduism, we receive another message. The earth, the water, the sun, the air, and space have always been sacred, not because they serve the needs of humans, but because humans cannot exist without them; humans are composed of the elements. Furthermore, the life of humans is the same life that is found in similar combinations of elements, whether insect, animal, or fish. To violate a snail is to literally violate oneself. To rationalize and develop an environmental ethics, the Asian world need not resort to risk potential analyses; it need only accurately and honestly assess the potential ravage to life forms that is caused by unregulated development. For an American, the loss of trees is caused by unregulated development. For an American, the loss of trees and lakes due to acid rain could be regarded with indifference. To an Indian, traditionally trained, such loss is a loss of that which composes oneself.

From the traditional Indian view, it need not be the case that all industrialization be eschewed. Gandhi himself proclaimed it helpful, perhaps even necessary, to accept machinery into his vision of village economy. However, in his time, when old-style colonialism was the issue, he asserted that such machines must be Indian machines, that, in a sense, they too must be of the village. Industrialization in the modern technological sense undoubtedly has assisted and will continue to assist the Indian population. However, it can and will remain viable only if the motivating ethic is in keeping with indigenous tradition. As long as the trend to industrialization proceeds in its ever-gobbling consumption of natural resources, both elemental and human, without regard for the wider consequences, it is doomed to repeated tragedy and suffering like that of Bhopal. However, if, as Gandhi has demonstrated is possible, the Indian psyche uses its own tradition and ethical conscience in its quest for development, a tradition and conscience rooted in nonviolence and respect for all forms of life, success in achieving and maintaining a balance between life needs and the needs of the earth can be met. And then, perhaps, India could provide a model for the West.

Introduction to article by His Holiness the Dalai Lama*

[*by Steven Rockefeller, from *Spirit and Nature*, pp. 110-111]

The first of the basic Buddhist precepts counsels those pursuing the path into liberation to avoid destroying life, and one of the most popular Buddhist scriptures, the *Mettasutta*, urges the faithful to "develop loving kindness for the entire world." These ethical teachings, reinforced by a worldview that emphasizes the interdependence of all beings and the immanence of the sacred, have generated much interest in Buddhism in this time of environmental crisis. The most widely known spokesperson for the Buddhist tradition in the world today is the Dalai Lama, whose teachings strive to develop in others a sense of universal responsibility, emphasizing a commitment to world peace, human rights, and protection of the environment.

Tenzin Gyatso was born into a Tibetan peasant family home, but at the age of two he was identified, in accordance with traditional Tibetan practices, as the reincarnation of his predecessor, the 13th Dalai Lama. Soon thereafter he entered a rigorous program of education and spiritual training, which led him to earn the *Geshe* degree, a doctorate in Buddhist philosophy. At the age of fifteen, before his formal education was complete, he was called to assume full political responsibility as head of the Tibetan government. He found his homeland facing a growing threat from China. When the situation worsened and the Chinese army occupied Tibet in 1959, he was forced into exile. Since then he has resided in Dharmsala, India, where he heads the Tibetan government-in-exile and presides over a large community of Tibetans.

In an effort to resolve differences with the Chinese government and to restore human rights and peace in Tibet, the Dalai Lama has proposed a Five Point Peace Plan. The central idea in his proposal is the recommendation that Tibet be transformed into a zone of *ahimsa*, a peace sanctuary. More specifically, this would mean withdrawal of all military forces from Tibet, establishment of democratic self-government, and the preservation of Tibet as a great natural park and wilderness sanctuary where plant and animal life are strictly protected. "It is my dream," writes the Dalai Lama, "that the entire Tibetan plateau should become a free refuge where humanity and nature can live in peace and in harmonious balance." He explains that the transformation of Tibet into a peace sanctuary in Asia would fulfill its historical role as a peaceful Buddhist nation and create a needed buffer region separating the rival powers of India and China.

In his article, the Dalai Lama describes the earth as our home and seeks to set forth a "practical ethic of caring for our home" grounded in the Buddhist understanding of interdependence. It is his view that the most important factor in developing an ethic of caring for the earth is the cultivation in individuals of an attitude of compassion. Compassion generates the sense of universal responsibility that is fundamental to the true nature of humanity. With the growth of this sense of responsibility, there also arises the hope, courage, joy, and inner peace needed to sustain a person engaged in the problems of the contemporary world.

A Buddhist Perspective on Nature

The Dalai Lama

Brothers and sisters, I am very happy to be here with you, to come to this beautiful place once more. I have enjoyed the last few days very much. The speeches from the leaders of the various traditions have been very impressive.

Although I have prepared a speech myself, a large number of people have come here today, and I think you may have different interests. This creates confusion in my mind right now; just what subject should I address to be most helpful to all of you?

The first thing that will relieve my small anxiety is to confess that I am not an expert or a specialist on ecology or the environment. So I will address a broader subject. And if you have come here with some expectation on that score, I can say that, essentially, I have nothing to offer you. I can simply try to share some of my own views and experiences, and then maybe some of you will find some benefit; or at least some new ideas to think about.

Now, first I will try to explain briefly the Buddhist attitude and approach to the environmental crisis. In dealing with this subject, I would like to divide my talk in three stages. First, I will talk about the Buddhist perception of nature and reality. Second, I will discuss what kind of ethical principle an individual should adopt, based on that view of reality and nature. Third, I will talk about what kind of right conduct, what kind of measures, individuals and society should take to restore and correct the degradation of nature and the earth, based on such an ethical principle.

When talking about developing a correct understanding or correct view of reality and nature, Buddhism emphasizes the application of reasoning and analysis. It talks about four avenues of reasoning or analysis through which one can develop a correct understanding of reality and nature. These four can be called natural, relational, functional, and logical avenues of reasoning. Reasoning and analysis have to take into account the natural laws of the universe, the interrelationships that exist in the universe, the functional properties of things in reality, and the processes of reason itself, with which it understands the universe.

First, one takes into account the fundamental laws of nature, such as the fact that things exist, the fact that matter differs from consciousness, the fact that mind exists in a certain way, and so on. Second, reason takes into account the interdependence between these various entities that exist in the world, and so on. Third, reason takes into account the functional properties that we see in reality, the properties which emerge as a consequence of the interaction between multiple factors. Fourth, based on these three levels of understanding nature, Buddhism emphasizes understanding the process of human reasoning and analysis itself. For example, reason can understand how reliable knowledge is generated through inference, either about the probable nature of a cause from the observed nature of its effect, or about a probably future state of affairs from an observed state of its cause. In short, while Buddhism is usually thought of as a religion, it is actually a way of thought that emphasized the necessity for human reason to be applied to human problems.

When talking about the fundamental nature of reality, one could sum up the entire understanding of that nature in a simple verse: "Form is emptiness, and emptiness is form" (the *Heart Sutra*). This simple line sums up the Buddhist understanding of the fundamental nature of reality.

In appearance, we see the world of existence and experience. In essence, all those things are empty of intrinsic reality, of independent existence.

Superficially, if we were to look at the words "emptiness" and "form" or "appearance," they might seem to be contradictory. If anything has appearance, how can it be empty? If anything is empty, how can it have a form or appearance? To overcome this contradiction, one must understand the meaning of emptiness to be interdependence. The meaning of interdependence is emptiness of independent existence. Precisely because things and events exist relatively and appear as having form, they are empty of independent existence.

Events and things come into being as a result of the aggregation of many factors—causes and conditions. But because they lack independent or absolute existence, it is possible for experiences such as our sufferings—which we do not desire—to come to a cessation. And because they lack independent or absolute existence, it is possible for pleasant experiences such as our happiness—which we do desire—to be created within ourselves.

Fundamental to attaining the Buddhist perception of reality, which ultimately is emptiness, is the understanding of relativity, the principle of interdependence. And the meaning of interdependence has three levels. At its subtlest level, it is the interdependence of things with thought and conceptual designations. At its middle level, it is the interdependence of parts and wholes. And at the surface level, it is interdependence of causes and effects.

I think there is a direct connection between the correct understanding of ecology and the natural environment and the Buddhist principle of interdependence in terms of causes and effects and in terms of parts and wholes, factors and aggregates. But the correct understanding of the subtlest level of interdependence—that of the interdependence of things and conceptual constructions—has more to do with maintaining the balance of the outer and the inner world, and with the purification of the inner world.

I believe that every individual living being, whether animal or human, has an innate sense of self. Stemming from that innate sense of self, there is an innate desire to enjoy happiness and overcome suffering. And this is something which is innate to all beings. I believe it is a natural phenomenon. But if we tried to examine why such innate faculties are there within living beings, I do not think we could ever find a convincing answer. I would rather stop there and say that it is a natural fact. Various different philosophies have tried to examine that nature of living beings. And still, after centuries, this is not yet finally solved. So I think it is better to accept this as something natural, as a reality.

Therefore, we can say that the purpose of life is happiness, joy, and satisfaction, because life itself, I think, exists on the ground of hope, on the basis of hope. And hope is, of course, for the better, for the happier. That is quite natural, isn't it? In that case, relations with one's fellow human beings—and also, animals, including insects (even those which sometimes seem quite troublesome)—should be based on the awareness that all of them seek happiness, and none of them wants suffering. All have a right to happiness, a right to freedom from suffering.

And generally speaking, all beings seem beautiful to us, beautiful birds, beautiful beasts. Their presence gives us some kind of tranquility, some kind of joy; they are like an ornament to our lives really. And then the forest, the plants, and the trees, all these natural things come together to make ours surroundings pleasant. All are heavily interdependent in creating our joy and happiness, in removing our sufferings.

Our human ancestors survived by depending on trees, on wood. Their fires depended on the wood. The trees gave them shelter and protection. When a dangerous animal threatened them, they could climb up to safety. Some trees bear beautiful flowers, which are ornaments, which they picked and wore in their hair, something like our modern jewelry. Then, of course, there's the fruit of the trees, and nuts, which are nourishing. And finally, of course, there are the sticks made from the branches; when someone attacks, it's a weapon; when you get older, it is a cane, like a reliable friend.

Such examples, I think, show the historical basis of human nature. Later, as human culture developed, we made something more beautiful out of it, something poetical. During our ancestors' time, human survival and welfare were very dependent on trees. But as society and culture became more developed and sophisticated, this dependence became less and less, the trees became the subject of poetry.

So, therefore, this shows that our very existence is something heavily dependent on the environment.

Now since we are seeking happiness and joy, we must be able to distinguish the different causes and conditions that lead to happiness and joy, causes both immediate and long-term. One finds that, although the ultimate aim of the major

world religions is the achievement of the happy life after death, eternal life, they
do not encourage their adherents to neglect the well-being of the present life.

The expressed aim of Buddhism is the purification and development of the
mind through mental training in order to attain supreme liberation. But the meditation manuals place great emphasis on finding an ideal environment for the
practice of training the mind because a cleaner environment does have a tremendous impact on one's spiritual progress. The Buddhist literature mentions the
sanctity of the environment as inspiring and blessing the practitioner, and in turn
the practitioner's spiritual realization blessing the environment. There is an exchange between human spirit and nature. In tune with such awareness, we find
in Buddhist practice specific rituals aimed at regenerating the vitality of the
earth, at purifying the environment, wherein certain precious materials are buried underground, and then consecration rituals are performed.

I think that in ancient time, the human ability to measure the imbalance of
nature was very limited—almost none. At that time, there was no need for worry
or concern. But today, the human ability to disturb the balance of nature is growing. World population has increased immeasurably. Due to many factors, nature,
even the Mother Planet herself, it seems, is showing us a red light. She is saying,
"Be careful, you should realize there are limits!"

Taking care of the planet is nothing special, nothing sacred or holy. It's just
like taking care of our own house. We have no other planet, no other house, except this one. Even if there are a lot of disturbances and problems, it is our only
alternative. We cannot go to any other planet. If the moon is seen from a dis-
tance, it appears quite beautiful. But if we go there to stay, I think, it would be
horrible. So, our blue planet is much better, much happier. Therefore, we have to
take care of our own place. This is not something special or holy. This is just a
practical fact!

Now I will go on to the second part of my talk, the development of an ethical principle based on the Buddhist understanding of reality and nature as emptiness and interdependence.

Essentially, nature's elements have secret ways of adapting. When something is damaged, another element helps out and improves the situation through
some kind of evolution. This is nature's way of adjustment. But then, human
intervention creates certain changes which do not give nature and its elements
time to cope. So the main troublemaker, the major cause of imbalance, is we
human beings ourselves. Therefore, the responsibility should be borne by us. We
must find some way to restrain our destructive habits.

We cause these problems mainly with our modern economy. With different
kinds of factories and chemicals, we have a strong negative impact on the balance of nature. The next question is, if that is the case, whether we have to stop
all factories, all chemicals. Of course, we cannot do that. While there are negative side effects, there are also tremendous benefits. True science and technology bring humanity a lot of benefit.

So what to do? We must use our human intelligence. And in some cases, we
must have more patience. We must cultivate more contentment. And we must

handle new progress and development in a proper way, keeping the side effects to a minimum. At the same time, we must take care of the earth and its basic elements in a more balanced way, no matter how expensive the cost. I think that's the only way.

Here I have come to the third part of my talk. Based on a practical ethic of caring for our home, grounded in our understanding of interdependence, what kind of measure can we take to correct these imbalances in nature?

Generally speaking, crises emerge as a consequence of certain causes or conditions. Principal among them is ignorance of the real situation. In order to overcome that, the most effective means is to develop knowledge and understanding.

Presently, older people like myself are speaking out about these dangers— but I think that is very limited in effect. The greater responsibility, I feel, lies with the scientists, especially those who are trained in this field. Through their research, with their experimental data, they should make clear the real long-term consequences of certain negative practices and positive measures. Scientists and environmental experts should prepare a very specific and detailed global study of the long-term dangers and benefits our society will face in the future.

Materials based on such studies should then be thoroughly learned by young students right from the start. Young children should take the environment into account when they study about geography, economics, or history. I feel it's very important to introduce ecology into the school curriculum, pointing out the environmental problems that the world currently faces. Even at a very early age, children should be exposed to the understanding and knowledge of the planetary environmental crisis. The various media—newspapers, television—all should be responsible for communicating the reality of this threatening situation.

In some cases, we might be able to overcome ignorance, understand reality, and reach the situation where everyone knows what's going on. But still we do not act to prevent disaster. Such a lack of will to act—in spite of having the knowledge and understanding—stems, I think, either from negligence (becoming totally oblivious to the crisis) or from discouragement (the feeling that "I have no ability, I simply cannot do anything").

I firmly believe that the most important factor is our attitude and human motivation—genuine human love, human kindness, and human affection. This is the key thing. That will help us to develop human determination also. Genuine love or compassion is not a feeling of lofty pity, sympathy tinged with contempt toward the other, a looking down on them; it is not like that. True love or compassion is actually a special sense of responsibility. A strong sense of care and concern for the happiness of the other, that is genuine. Such true love automatically becomes a sense of responsibility.

So, how should we develop compassion? How should we expand our love? First, it is very important to know that within the meaning of "love" is often merely blind love, or blind attachment. In many cases, it involves unconscious projections on the other, possessiveness, and desire; it is usually not at all good. There is a second level of love or compassion, which is a kind of condescending pity. But that is not really positive compassion. We feel genuine compassion and love not just for beings close to us, but for all persons and animals. Such true compassion develops from the recognition that everyone does not want suffering and does want happiness, just like us. When we really feel that, we feel that they have every right to be happy and every right to overcome suffering. Realizing that, we naturally develop a genuine concern for their suffering and their right to be free from it.

We can feel this kind of genuine love for others no matter what their attitude toward us. That love is steady; so long as any person or being suffers, we feel responsible, even if he or she is our enemy. Love mixed with attachment makes us concerned for beings close to us. That kind of love is biased and always narrow and limited. But genuine love is much wider and stronger. And it can be developed.

If we analyze the situation in various ways, we can develop a firm conviction about the need for such a mental attitude, even out of self-interest. In our daily life, it is the energy of genuine love and compassion that is the source of hope, the source of happiness, the source of joy, and the source of inner strength.

When we have that kind of love with its strong sense of responsibility, we will never lose our hope or our determination. The more we are challenged by negative forces, the more determination we will develop. So it is really the source of every success. That is what I always feel.

In our daily lives, we love smiles. I especially love a genuine smile, not a sarcastic smile, or a diplomatic smile, which sometimes even increases suspicion. But I consider the genuine smile something really precious. It is the great bridge of communication. Whether you know the same language or not, whether you are from the same culture, or nation, or race—all that is secondary. The basic thing is to realize that the other is a human being, a gentle human being who wants happiness and does not want suffering, just like ourselves. At that basic level, we just smile—we can exchange smiles. Then immediately the barrier is broken and we feel close.

After all, a human being is a social animal. I often tell my friends that there is no need to study philosophy or other complicated subjects. Just look at those innocent insects, like ants or bees. I am very fond of honey—so I am always exploiting the bees' hard work. Therefore, I have a special interest in the lives of bees. I learned many things about them and developed a special relationship with them. They amaze me. They have no religion, no constitution, and no police force, but their natural law of existence requires harmony, and they have a natural sense of responsibility. They follow nature's system.

So what is wrong with us, we human beings? We have such a great intelligence, our human intelligence, our human wisdom. But I think we often use our human intelligence in the wrong way, we turn it in the wrong direction. As a result, in a way we are doing certain actions which are essentially contrary to our basic human nature. And here I always feel that basic human nature is compassion or affection.

This is quite simple. If we look closely at the beginning of human life, at the conception of a child, we see that sexual relations and the forming of a family are connected with real love. From the biological perspective, according to natural law, the main purpose is reproduction. And I think that the beneficial kind of love—even of sexual love—is love with a sense of care and responsibility. Mad love is not lasting, I think, if it lacks a sense of responsibility.

Look at those beautiful wild birds. When two birds come together, it is to build a nest and raise their young. When they have chicks, the male and the female both assume the same responsibility to feed the little ones. Sometimes mad love is just wild, just like dogs, completely careless about the consequences. I think it is not very good for people. If that was all there was to it, there would be no use for marriage. And yet look how people consider the marriage ceremony something important. If we really consider it important, then we should have the love that is a sense of responsibility. If we did develop that, I think there would be fewer divorces, wouldn't there? Marriages would last longer—I think until death.

At any rate, we can see that human life begins with affection, with love, a sense of responsibility and care. We are in the mother's womb for many months. During this time the mother's mental calmness is said to be a very important factor for the healthy development of the unborn child. And after birth, according to some neurobiologists, the first few weeks are the most important period for the healthy development of the child's brain. And they say that, during that time, the mother's actual physical touch is a crucial factor. This does not come from religious scripture or ideology. It is from scientific observation.

Therefore, I believe that this human body itself very much appreciates affection. The first action of the child is the sucking of the mother's milk. And the mother, in spite of pain and exhaustion, is very willing to give milk to her child. So milk is a profound symbol of affection. Without mother's milk we cannot survive. That is human nature.

During the process of education, it is quite easy to notice how much better we learn from a teacher who not only teaches us but also shows a real concern for our welfare, who cares about our future. The lessons of such a teacher go much deeper in our mind than lessons received from a teacher who just explains about the subject without any human affection. This again shows the power of affection in nature.

The art of medicine is another good example. During this trip, I visited a hospital in New York about a problem in my left nostril. The doctor who examined me and removed the blockage was so gentle and careful, in addition to having a beautiful machine. His face was full of life—and he had a genuine smile. In spite of some pain from that small operation, I felt very fresh, quite happy and confident. In some cases when we visit doctors, they may be very professional, but if they show no human affection, we feel anxious, suspicious, and unsure how it will turn out. Haven't we all noticed that?

In our old age we again reach a stage where we come to depend heavily on others' affection. We appreciate even the slightest affection and concern. And even when we face death, on our last day, even though all efforts are now exhausted, though there is no hope, still, if some genuine friend is there at our bedside, we feel much happier. Although there is no more time to do anything, we still feel much happier—because of human nature.

So, from the beginning of human life to the end of human life, during all those years, it is clear that human affection is the key for human happiness, human survival, and human success. What do you think? This is how I feel.

Therefore, affection, love, and compassion—they are not a matter of religion. Various religions do teach us the importance of love and compassion because the basic aim of religions is the support and benefit of human beings. Since human nature is love, since genuine love and compassion are so important for life, every religion, in spite of different philosophies, traditions, and ideologies, teaches us about love and compassion. But human affection as essential for human nature is something deeper than matters of religious belief or institutional affairs. It is even more basic for human survival and success than any particular religion.

Therefore, I always used to tell people that whether they are believers or nonbelievers, that's up to them. From a certain point of view, religion is a little bit of a luxury. If you have religion, that's very good. But even without religion, you can survive, you can manage to live and even sometimes succeed. But not without human affection; without love, we cannot survive. Therefore, affection, love, and compassion, they are the deepest aspect of human nature.

Some of you here may doubt this. You may feel that anger and hatred are also part of human nature. Yes, of course anger is a human habit. But if we carefully investigate, I think we will find the dominant force of the human mind is affection.

As I mentioned earlier, when we are first born, if the mother feels the agitation of resentment or anger toward the child, then her milk may not flow freely. I noticed when I visited Ladakh that sometimes when people milk their cow, the cow's calf is brought in front of the cow first. This way they cheat the cow; in her mind, she is giving milk to her own baby. So that shows that there is a natural condition where without a tender loving feeling of closeness, the milk may not come. So milk is the result of affection and is blocked by anger.

Again I have another reason, if we look carefully at daily life. When something happens which horrifies our minds, a murder case or terrorist attack, it is immediately reported in all the news because an event like this makes such a forceful impression in the mind. And yet every day thousands and millions of undernourished children are given food; they are nourished and they survive another day. But no one reports that because it is something normal; it should be a routine happening. We take it for granted. These facts also demonstrate our human nature and that affection is something normal. Killing and other actions born of anger and hatred are unusual for us. And so such unfortunate events strike our minds more forcefully. The basic human nature is gentle. And so I feel that there is a real possibility to promote and develop human affection on the global level. It is not unrealistic, because it is the most important part of human nature.

Each of us is an individual, naturally a part of humanity. So human effort must begin with our individual initiatives. Each of us should have a strong sense of the responsibility to create our own small part of a positive atmosphere. At the same time, we have more powerful social methods today with which to channel individual human insight and inspiration and thus to have a wider impact. There are different organizations on the national and international levels, governments, and United Nations organizations. These are powerful channels through which to implement new insights, to mobilize new inspirations.

This kind of conference is very helpful to such an end, though it would be unrealistic to expect that a few conferences could achieve any sort of complete solution. That's expecting too much. But, the constant effort of deep thought and broad discussion is very useful and worthwhile.

Introduction to article by Susan Darlington

Over 95% of the population of Thailand is Buddhist. The "brand" of Buddhism found there is Theravada, the oldest form of Buddhism practiced and one which regards the figure and the teachings (*dhamma* or *dharma*) of the Buddha as guides and as an inspiration toward living a faithful Buddhist life. In this version of Buddhism, the Buddha "points" the follower in the proper direction, but it is up to him or her to achieve the spiritual goal of enlightenment.

Professor Darlington's article is based on her extensive research and personal interviews in Thailand over a number of years. In it, she places the Thai environmental movement, and the emergence first of "development monks" in the early 1970s and then of "environmentalist monks" in the late 20th century, in historical, political, economic, and social context: The history of the government's economic and environmental policy, and of the relationship between religion and that government, are discussed. This is followed by not only a description of the ways in which the dominant religion of the state was co-opted to support and legitimize the state's policies, but also a description of the dissent of a minority of monks who sought/seek alternative development.

She then reveals two key examples of environmentalist monks—Phrakhru Pitak Nanthakhun and Phra Somit—and discusses their backgrounds and the key experiential and religious reasons they became involved in environmental issues, most prominently, deforestation. Dr. Darlington's article illustrates the why's, what's, and how's of Buddhism-in-action or "engaged Buddhism" in a specific region and society.

Rethinking Buddhism and Development: *The Emergence of Environmentalist Monks in Thailand*

Susan M. Darlington

In 1991, the Thai Buddhist monk, Phrakhru Pitak Nanthakhun, sponsored a tree ordination in Nan Province. The ritual—conducted by twenty northern Thai monks and attended by close to 200 villagers, district officials, and journalists—formally established and sanctified a protected community forest for ten adjoining villages. The hour-long ceremony included chanting, sanctification of water, and wrapping a monk's orange robes around the largest remaining tree in the forest. The ten village headmen drank the holy water to seal their pledge to protect the forest. This ritual was one of numerous tree ordinations conducted by Buddhist monks in the 1990s in an effort to preserve the nation's rapidly-depleting forest and protect people's livelihoods within it.

"Environmentalist monks" (*phra nak anuraksa* in Thai) form a small percentage of the total number of monks in Thailand. Nevertheless, their actions are visible in Thai society. They tackle urgent and controversial issues, such as deforestation and the construction of large dams, using modified Buddhist rituals and an ecological interpretation of Buddhist teachings.

The effectiveness of environmentalist monks' projects remains unclear. Because these monks have only been active in Thailand [for a relatively-brief period of time], not enough time has passed to assess projects aimed at stopping deforestation or cleaning polluted rivers. Their projects do not have sufficient scope to change what most environmentalists perceive as the destructive patterns of deforestation and growth-oriented economic and industrial development that have been dominant in Thailand since the 1960s.

Despite their small numbers and limited effectiveness, this group represents a case of people within a specific cultural setting who are implementing their own environmental concepts. They reinvent human relationships with nature in the face of what has been criticized as the capitalization of nature worldwide. Their environmental seminars and their relations with local people illustrate the processes through which this small group of monks challenges the dominant trend of "ecological capital" [a term coined by Arturo Escobar in *Liberation Ecologies* in 1996]. Despite a historical link between the Buddhist *Sangha* [the community of monks] and the Siamese [Thai] state, these monks reject the state's definition of development and how it is implemented.

A high degree of environmental degradation has accompanied the government's growth and export-oriented development policies. The Thai forest has been cut down at one of the fastest rates in Asia. According to official figures, forest cover in Thailand decreased from 72% of the total land in 1938 [about 75 years ago] to 53% in 1961 [about 50 years ago] and 29% in 1985 [about 25 years ago]. Most environmental non-governmental organizations [NGO's] estimate that less than 15% of the country's total land area can be considered forest today. Activist monks join a growing, popular environmental movement that questions the government's priorities and policies.

The contemporary development concept was first formulated in the mid-1800's, when King Mongkut brought his kingdom into the global economy and restructured the Buddhist *Sangha* to legitimize the central government. Changing Thai governments have continued to use Buddhism to support their development agendas, especially since the 1960's. This process resulted in the rise of independent "development monks" in the 1970's and "environmental monks" in the late 1980's who challenged the government's concept of development, Buddhism's legitimation of it, and the suffering that they believed it caused the Thai people. Ironically, engaged Buddhism in Thailand emerged out of the same political-economic situation and close relationship with the state that it seeks to change . . .

Development in Thailand

Siam, as Thailand was formerly known, remained a small, relatively-isolated kingdom until 1855, when the Bowring Treaty with Great Britain formally brought it into the emerging global economy. Even as the Siamese attempted to limit foreign access to their markets, the colonial economies being developed in neighboring countries forced them to rethink their relations with the international community and begin to modernize. Initiated by King Mongkut [Rama IV, who reigned from 1851–1868], Siam introduced modern scientific concepts, economic practices, and education.

Mongkut also instituted religious reform in the 1830s and 1840s, and established the Thammayut Order of the *Sangha*. Similar to the modernization of other aspects of Thai society that Mongkut initiated, he rationalized the religion, aiming to eliminate practices that he felt were too ritualistic, metaphysical, or overly-influenced by local or regional culture . . .

Mongkut linked the *Sangha* hierarchy with the absolute monarchy based in Bangkok, using it to legitimize the central government and weaken the influence of regional forms of religion and the power of regional political leaders. The legitimizing role that the *Sangha* played toward the state was strengthened as Bangkok expanded its control to the peripheral regions, using wandering forest monks to forge relations with remote rural peoples. During the modernization period, Siam—renamed Thailand in 1932—established the three-fold concept of religion, monarchy, and nation, formalizing the connection between religion and state even further . . .

[Successive] governments . . . have continued aggressive industrial and export-oriented development and agricultural intensification policies. The results have been mixed: Thailand's growth until the economic crisis was phenomenal, but the rate of environmental degradation, especially forest loss and pollution levels, was among the highest in Asia. The gap between rich and poor widened, and consumerism spread, symbolized by the growth of malls and McDonald's restaurants. Rural people's quality of life deteriorated as they moved from subsistence to market farming or left the countryside to seek work in urban factories.

"Development Monks"

Not all members of the *Sangha* agreed with either the government's development agenda or the involvement of monks in it. Beginning in the early 1970s, a handful of monks began independent rural development projects based on their interpretations of Buddhist teachings and in opposition to the capitalism promoted by the government. Of particular concern was the impact of the government's rapid development program on rural people's lives, and because of the government's emphasis on Buddhism as a form of nationalism, the erosion of traditional local Buddhist values. These monks feared the effects of growing consumerism and the dependence of farmers on outside markets. Working in specific villages and addressing localized concerns and problems, these self-proclaimed "development monks" began conducting alternative development projects.

One of the first development monks, Phra Dhammadilok, formed his own NGO—the Foundation of Education and Development of Rural Areas. . . . He realized that if people are hungry, cold, and sick, they will not and cannot devote their energy toward religious ends. Similarly, without spiritual development and commitment, they cannot overcome material suffering . . . [His] projects, located in over 35 villages today, include rice banks, buffalo banks (which provide buffaloes for poor farmers to plow their fields), credit unions, small revolving funds for agricultural development initiatives, integrated agriculture projects, and training for rural women in traditional handicrafts and sewing to enable them to supplement their agricultural incomes.

Unlike most government programs, the projects of Phra Dhammadilok and other development monks are aimed at local, rather than national or regional development. They respond to immediate needs identified by the rural peoples themselves. Most of the development monks are from the areas in which they work, making them aware of the problems that rapid economic change has brought to rural people. They initiate projects designed for a specific location and problem using local cultural concepts and beliefs rather than pulling people into a national agenda that often ignores their needs and wants . . .

Both NGOs and development monks emerged because of concern over the negative impacts of government development policies toward Thai society, culture, and environment. Together they have fostered the rise of a national environmental movement.

Rise of the Environmental Movement

While development monks worked on a local level, the environmental movement grew on a national level in response to the government's economic development agenda. Many of the NGOs that were engaged in a search for alternative forms of development moved into environmental activism because of their concerns about the rate of environmental destruction and degradation caused by the policies of the central government.

The causes for environmental degradation in Thailand are numerous, multifaceted, and virtually impossible to verify, but the coincidence of the nation's rapid economic growth from the 1960s to the mid-1990s and its high rate of forest loss and environmental problems during the same period fuel fierce debate. The government, supported by international organizations such as the World Bank, argues that environmental destruction is primarily due to poverty, making economic growth imperative to solving environmental problems. Environmentalists, on the other hand, point to the inequalities underlying the government's development agenda as the root of much of the country's poverty. The government's policies, they argue, further promote destruction of the forest by encouraging agricultural intensification and capital growth through the exploitation of natural resources. The arguments are complex and beyond the scope of this article, but it is critical to note the range of positions surrounding environmental issues, even within the environmental movement.

The case of forest reserves and national parks illustrates the complexity of environmentalism in Thailand. Forests represent a major natural resource for the nation. Thailand invested heavily in logging until a ban was passed [20 years ago] after 300 people died in floods caused by deforestation and erosion. Debates will range concerning the best way to manage the country's forests and the role of the local people. . . . On one side, local peoples living within the forests are blamed for destructive agricultural practices such as the slash-and-burn method. Advocates of this perspective argue that to preserve the remaining forest land, these people should be moved out of the forest and trained in more environmentally-friendly methods. Others argue that it is the local people who can best look after the forest because their livelihoods depend on the natural resources that they contain. Therefore, rather than moving them out and allowing illegal loggers, hunters, and developers to take advantage of the changes, forest dwellers should be granted titles to the land that they have used for generations.

The environmentalist Buddhist monks are also caught-up in this debate. The majority takes the position that local forest dwellers will best protect the forest. A few others argue strongly that people must be moved from forests . . . if there is to be any chance of protecting the remaining forested land . . .

Thai environmentalism cannot be simplified into a two-sided debate. It entails multiple perspectives . . . [those of] rural farmers, whose livelihoods depend on a healthy environment [and] . . . middle-class Thais . . . [who] see the need to protect and preserve nature from human impact. Most farmers see themselves as caretakers intimately familiar with and dependent upon a natural environment that includes people as a part of a whole ecological system. Activist monks often use the latter argument as an example of the Buddhist concept of dependent origination [pratityasamutpada], showing the interdependence of all things . . .

Emergence of Environmentalist Monks

It is within the context of debates over development and the rise of a diverse yet influential environmental movement that the self-proclaimed "environmentalist monks" emerged. Just as the environmental movement in Thailand grew out of the concerns of the NGOs about the ecological impact of government development policies and global ecological capitalism, the work of environmentalist monks evolved from that of independent development monks with concerns about local people's lives and spirituality . . .

The work of two monks in Nan Province [northern Thailand] illustrates the process and the potential of the knowledge created by environmentalist monks. The first monk is Phrakhru Pitak Nanthakhun. He was born and raised in the village of Giew Muang, deep in the mountainous forest north of Nan City. His introduction to both environmental concerns and Buddhism arose out of an incident that occurred when he was a child. Phrakhru witnessed his father shoot a mother monkey while hunting. Its baby clung to the mother's body, allowing it to be captured. For three days, it cried from its cage, and when the boy finally released it, it went, still crying, straight to the skin of its mother hanging out to dry. This experience contributed not only to Phrakhru Pitak's later conservation work, but also was part of the reason that he was ordained as a Buddhist novice [a beginner-monk, undergoing a probationary period] and has remained in the Sangha for almost 30 years. He realized that the teachings of the Buddha [about pain and suffering, about compassion and non-violence] could prevent such human-induced suffering.

Growing out of his childhood experience with the baby monkey, Phrakhru Pitak incorporated a message of the environmental responsibility of humans into his teachings. The urgency of preaching an environmental ethic became clearer to him as he witnessed the continual deforestation of his mountainous province. This was caused by logging concessions, illegal logging, slash-and-burn agriculture, overuse of the land by villagers, and the introduction of cash cropping [growing products not for private sustenance but for public sale; the size of the harvest then often becomes the highest and only priority, overriding concerns about the quality of and damage to the land].

. . . Phrakhru Pitak realized that preaching alone was not enough, that he needed to become actively engaged in conservation work. He visited Phrakhru Manas, the monk generally credited with first performing tree ordinations to raise awareness of the value of the forests. Symbolically ordaining large trees in an endangered forest by wrapping monks' orange robes around them serves several purposes: First, the action draws attention to the threat of deforestation. Second, the ritual provides the opportunity for the ecology monks and the laity who work with them to teach about the impact of environmental destruction and the value and means of conserving nature. Finally, the monks use the ritual to teach the *Dhamma* [or *Dharma*, the teachings of the Buddha] and to stress its relevance in a rapidly-changing world.

After visiting Phrakhru Manas, Phrakhru Pitak returned to Nan and began actively teaching villagers about environmental conservation, presenting slide shows, and holding discussions with people about the problems that they face due to deforestation. He helped his home village establish a community forest encompassing about 400 acres of land. The community forest was officially consecrated, and the villagers' commitment to preserving it was marked by the ordination of the largest remaining tree. Letters were sent to the surrounding villages announcing the creation of the protected area and making clear that it was forbidden to cut trees or hunt within it. The village also performed a ceremony asking for spiritual help to assist them in protecting the forest and its wildlife.

Phrakhru Pitak's work is not limited to his home village, but instead is constantly being expanded. He has sponsored *pha pa* ceremonies, which are traditionally used to give "forest robes" to monks, but in these cases they include giving seedlings for reforestation. Lay people make religious merit through their donations and participation. [He] held an adapted traditional ceremony to preserve and lengthen the life of the Nan River in conjunction with a seminar to highlight the problems of desiccation and pollution that the province faces. A fish sanctuary was established at the site of the ceremony as well. Over 39 community forests and 100 fish sanctuaries have been established by Phrakhru Pitak's NGO—the We Love Nan Province Foundation.

Phrakhru Pitak emphasizes basic Buddhist principles such as dependent origination and an interpretation of the Buddha's life that highlights a close relationship with the forest. . . . Phrakhru Pitak also encourages sustainable development practices such as integrated agriculture and growing food for subsistence rather than for sale. Villagers are willing to try his approaches because of their respect for him as a monk and their awareness of his concern for their well-being. He is outspoken in his criticism of government-sponsored economic development promoting cash crops and the use of chemical fertilizers . . .

Phra Somkit [is] the second example of an environmentalist monk. . . . Similarly concerned with deforestation around his village, Phra Somkit began nearly twenty years ago protecting the village's forest. He went *bindabat* for forest, which is traditionally the practice of going on alms rounds providing lay people with the opportunity to make merit through giving food to monks. Phra Somkit's innovation entailed offering villagers the opportunity to make merit by donating land to the village temple. His father was the first to make an offering, presenting approximately one acre of hilly land that been denuded through intensive cultivation of corn as a cash crop.

As a means to protect the forest, Phra Somkit began a model integrated-agriculture farm on land belonging to his temple. With the help of his younger brother, he maintains two fish ponds, raises free-range chickens, and plants natural rice plots behind the temple. . . . He uses no chemical fertilizers, pesticides, or herbicides to demonstrate the benefits of natural farming to the villagers. On the land donated by his father, Phra Somkit has allowed the forest to regenerate naturally. In the time since the original gift, the forest has again grown dense . . .

Phra Somkit strongly believes in the importance of education in the protection of the natural environment. Using the mountainous terrain surrounding the village, he regularly takes children on ecology meditation walks. He works with them to consider the value of the plants and wildlife with which they share their environment. His belief is that through teaching children about human responsibility toward nature, they will take their lessons home and teach their parents. Phra Somkit undertakes all this work as part of what he perceives as his own responsibility as a Buddhist monk.

Conclusion

Both Phra Somkit and Phrakhru Pitak illustrate ways in which environmentalist monks respond to changing national, regional, and global agendas concerning development and the environment within local contexts. Their motivation comes from witnessing environmental degradation and the suffering that it creates. Actively seeking-out the causes of this suffering has led them to redefine the underlying concepts of development and progress. Their awareness has led them to re-examine Buddhist teachings to support their work

. . .

While environmentalist monks do not form a united, coherent movement, the collective implication of their work illustrates the concept of "liberation ecology" [the emancipatory potential of environmental ideas]. . . . The impact of their activism to challenge Thai Buddhists to rethink their religion, their society, and their place in both the political and the natural world cannot be denied.

Introduction to article by Gopinder Kaur Sagoo

The fifth largest of the world's religions, Sikhism began in the fifteenth century in an area of northern India called the Punjab. Sikhism contains elements of Hinduism (e.g., karma and reincarnation) and Islam (e.g., monotheism and God's omnipotence), though it is a distinct religious tradition.

Sikhs follow the teachings of eleven gurus, beginning with the founder, Nanak (1469–1539). The tenth guru, Gobind Singh, transferred his authority in 1708 to *Adi Granth* (the original sacred writings of Sikhism), which become known as the eleventh guru, *Guru Granth Sahib*. This is Sikhism's holy Scripture.

Sikhs are universalists, seeing revelation and truth in all religious traditions; they have consistently stood for religious liberty and tolerance, and historically have been a bastion of resistance to oppression. Numerous times, they have suffered torture and death for this resistance and for their principles. In Sikhism, women ideally enjoy equality, full respect, and freedom of participation.

The purpose of life, according to Sikhism, is to realize God within the world through the everyday practices of work, worship, and charity.

In Gopinder Kaur Sagoo's article, she shares very personally how her faith orients her toward the natural world. By tapping Sikh scriptures and sayings, she connects her religion's sense of relationship to the environment with Sikh visionaries' and activists' endeavors to improve its condition.

Our Environment and Us: *A Sikh Perspective*

Gopinder Kaur Sagoo

Pavan Guru, pani pita, mata dharat mahat
Divas ra-t dui da-i da-ya, khelai sagal jaga

"Air is our Guru, water our father, and great earth is our mother;
Day and night are the male and female nurses, in whose lap the whole world plays"

Growing up as a Sikh child, these were some of the first lines from *Gurbani*, Sikh sacred verse, which became familiar to me, signaling the close of "*Jap Ji Sahib*," our early morning prayer. As I absorbed their rhyme and rhythm, it was probably the simple imagery echoing a child's eye view of the world which captivated me most. It expresses the state of being "a child of the universe," by personifying nature and the elements into the figures of Guru, father ("*pita*") and mother ("*mata*"), and those who nurse us in our infancy—the central personalities who nurture and guide our growing bodies, minds and spirits. Such relationships are more than functional; they are held in balance by the twin qualities of love and respect and are marked by a capacity for self-sacrifice. Water and earth, father and mother, bring forth and sustain new life; the air too sustains us, and transmits to us the Guru's sacred words, which are capable of transforming us.

I begin with this personal recollection because, by illuminating our sense of relationship to the environment, it sets the tone for the reflections which are to follow, based on conversations I have had with Sikhs who can be described as environmental visionaries and activists. What I hope emerges is an understanding of how Sikh scripture and sayings help to give meaning, purpose, value and commitment to such endeavors, and of how this transformative dimension can be neglected when we attempt only to recognize the 'mechanics' of any faith tradition—be it viewed from the inside out or the outside in.

Whatever our background or worldview, all of us are enmeshed in a web of systems and forces whose by-product is environmental harm on an unprecedented scale. From a purely secular perspective, it is nonsensical to continue in this way, and such behavior does not become us as humans. What does a faith-inspired perspective bring to this base-level understanding, and how does this filter down to those who inherit, associate with, or commit to the Sikh faith? What is it like to look at one's environment through Sikh eyes, more particularly through those eyes to which the "eyeliner" of the Guru's wisdom has been applied?

"A person of faith cannot help but feel a deep sense of connection, love, awe and respect for the environment," remarks Bhai Sahib Mohinder Singh, who serves as spiritual leader of Guru Nanak Nishkam Sewak Jatha (GNNSJ), a Sikh registered charity active in building partnerships with both civic and faith organizations to work towards sustainable peace, locally and globally:

> Our central belief is *Ik Oankar*: the One Creator pervades all creation. *Apin-ai ap sajio, apin-ai rachio naou; duyi kudrat saji-ai, kar asan dittho chaou.* . . . *Asa di Var*, the early morning spiritual ballad, tells us that upon creating Himself, God created *nam*, the divine name—the first expression of His sacred presence. Secondly He created *kudrat* or nature, which is sustained and totally infused by *nam*. So, the Creator observes creation, and dwells within it. Both are interconnected. You will find this is something stressed especially by the Eastern faiths. One cannot help but live in gratitude and respect for the gifts of nature which are marks of God's grace. *Balihari kudrat vasia tera ant na jae lakhia.* . . . I am totally indebted to you, Oh Infinite Lord, who dwells within nature and whose limits cannot be told

Let us think about this word "environment." I understand it comes from the French *environs*—our surroundings. This includes not only the physical landscape, but the people and creatures around us. We must care for it, not simply in a mechanical way, but through an attitude of love based on *sarbat da bhalla* or seeking the "well-being of all." We must think about the "ecology" of our relationships and attitudes towards each other. Industry creates toxins that pollute the earth, but we also create toxins which pollute the environment of our minds and bodies, through our selfish and ignorant tendencies. *Haumai dhirag rog hai, daru bhi is mahi.* . . . Gurbani [Sikh sacred verse] tells me the human ego, *haumai*, is an innate part of us, but it can afflict us like chronic disease. Faith is the antidote which uplifts us and unlocks our capacity for *deya* (compassion, human kindness). Then *deya* is not merely an "obligation," but a "quality" of our being. This is probably why you find that faith-based organizations are able to achieve tremendous things with few material resources.

My mind flits to a painting which several years ago won the Westminster Faith Exchange Arts Competition for the 15–19 age group, under the theme, "What prayer means to me." In it, young Sikh artist Jaskirat Singh Thethy depicted the Earth supported by the cupped hands of "deya" and "santokh," or compassion and contentment, inspired by the imagery of a verse in *Jap Ji Sahib*. These qualities sustain us spiritually as a human entity; they also hold in place our very existence as a planetary entity. I am reminded in turn of Oxfam's recent television campaign, calling on us to "Be Humankind." A little old lady going about her daily business starts to notice words representing global problems manifesting themselves as bugs around street corners, scurrying towards the giant monster of injustice. Compelled to act with her conscience awakened, she releases a lion-like roar, emitting rays of light, which are joined by those of others, bringing rainbows of hope to an otherwise gloomy planet.

"To be a person of faith is to be duty-bound to care for creation," continues Bhai Sahib Mohinder Singh:

> You know, I rarely use this word "Sikhism". I prefer to talk of Sikh *dharam*. "Faith" or "religion," I find, are inadequate translations. *Dharam* for me is a self-acknowledged duty towards Creator and creation. You cannot love one without loving the other. And *Jap Ji Sahib* tells me to see this whole planet as a *dharamsal*—like a school to practice *dharam*, a giant place of worship, which we visit as spiritual travelers. Our goal is to generate spiritual wealth, in the form of divine attributes, with which to build wholesome lives and serve creation. These are the only "souvenirs" we take with us on our return home. Instead, society glorifies the amassing of material wealth, thoughtlessly and wastefully, which causes destruction. We suffer from a lot of ignorance also, not only about our individual actions. Many times I wonder about the sheer scale of undisclosed ecological damage caused by modern warfare and nuclear testing. We have had Hiroshima and Nagasaki, plus numerous nuclear testing during the Cold War; we hear about the human death toll in Iraq, but know very little about the impact of war on its ecology.

In 2006, Bhai Sahib participated as an NGO and faith representative at a UN conference to discuss challenges to fulfilling the eight Millennium Development Goals, agreed by 189 countries to overcome key problems we face on a global scale. There, he stressed there was a missing ninth Millennium Development Goal: The spiritual regeneration of the individual "to ignite the nucleus of divine power latent within each of us"—a prerequisite for harnessing the degree of altruism and commitment needed to attain these goals and overcome the gridlock caused by apathy and selfishness. "*Dharam* means we have a duty of care," Bhai Sahib continues. "As rulers and caretakers of the planet, we must strive to be noble, responsible, humble and wise. My turban and kirpan [religious knife] are constant reminders of this," he notes, pointing out the distinguishing marks of his identity as a Sikh.

I reflect on the character of the *sant-sipahi*, the saint-soldier of Sikh tradition—one who battles with inner demons to secure the victory of saintliness, which in turn motivates and guides thoughts and actions in the field of life. This is reflected again in the two outer *kirpans* of the *khanda* emblem, featured on the *nishan sahib* flag which identifies a Sikh *gurdwara* [place of worship]. They proclaim the concept of *miri-piri,* that all secular power (*miri*) must be balanced and tempered by the strength of spiritual wisdom and values (*piri*). Freedom and sovereignty are made noble because of this; without this equilibrium, our personal liberty and socio-political systems fall prey to the workings of selfishness, greed, ignorance, and an absence of ethics. *Miri-piri* puts a concern for ethical and spiritual standards at the heart of all human activity.

Today, however, we are easily deluded by that which on the surface seems benign: The slickness of marketing and our own comfort zones mask the economic, agricultural, industrial, and other forms of exploitation taking place on a global scale. This, I sometimes think, is the sophisticated face of *maya,* worldly delusion which takes us away from the true nature of things. Most of us, Sikhs included, find ourselves enmeshed within such a delusion. Sikhs tend to inherit their faith through birth, since it is not a proselytizing religion. Through our particular history, we have faced various challenges to "learning about" and "learning from" our Sikh spiritual heritage, learning which might allow us to harness this heritage to heighten awareness of what it means to be part of the environment and compel us to do more to respect and protect it. Still, the notion of environment runs strong within the Sikh psyche—the fact that faith is not only in one's "head" or "heart," but is expressed through one's lifestyle, what one consumes, one's gestures, speech, and appearance: The wholeness of the 'environment' of the individual and community within which its spiritual character unfolds and grows.

Part of the Sikh lifestyle (especially of an initiated *Khalsa* practitioner) includes abstinence from nicotine, drugs, alcohol, and, according to many committed practitioners of the faith, from food derived from the slaughter of animals. The body is talked of as a home, temple, or even a universe unto itself, and regarded as a sacred space. The turban honors the seat of wisdom within the human frame; the wearing of the Five Ks [*Kesh* (uncut hair); *Kara* (steel bracelet); *Kangha* (wooden comb); *Kachera* (cotton underwear); and *Kirpan* (steel knife/sword)] inspires courage to uphold goodness, based on compassion and dignity (*Kirpan*), commitment to the Creator and to ethical behavior (*Kara*), modesty and self-restraint (*Kachera*), saintliness and a spirit of harmony with the natural order (*Kesh*), whilst maintaining tidiness, order and seeking purity (*Kangha*). Our inherent dignity as humans and capacity for wise rule is reflected in the names Singh and Kaur, both associated with royalty [prince and princess, respectively]. Such qualities and principles have resonance with an environmental consciousness and, who knows, if we were to try and visualize an "eco-warrior," the image of the *Khalsa* might provide some interesting food for thought.

"To be 'environmentally-friendly' is too lukewarm a concept now," concludes Bhai Sahib Mohinder Singh.

Circumstances will demand us to become more active defenders of our environment. For this, we need to transform our mindsets, our whole planetary consciousness, and education plays an important role.

Let us try to teach ecology early and reduce the ignorance caused by excessive consumption and urbanization, and also learn from our grandparents, who knew the art of being resourceful and recycling.

Education lies at the heart of the ceaseless environmental work of Pardeep Singh Rai. Landscape gardener, educator and activist, he is a rare voice in the United Kingdom Sikh community devoted to raising environmental awareness and introducing practical change, which he does by drawing on his spiritual, cultural and, indeed, agricultural heritage as a Sikh and a Panjabi. He is also founder of DEEP, Defenders of the Ecology and Environment of the Panjab, and campaigns to bring attention to the ecocide of the "land of five rivers" (from "panj," five, and "ab," water), the birthplace of Sikh tradition.

Reports on the environmental degradation faced by the region, detailing forces which are transforming this once fertile "bread basket of India" into barren desert, can be found online in news from Birmingham Friends of the Earth and the Refugee Project. Pardeep Singh is also coordinator of the Environmental Group for the Panjabis in the Britain All-Party Parliamentary Group which has met on issues such as the "Pesticide Dilemma." "There are a few Panjab-based Sikhs committed to environmental work in the region," points out Pardeep, "such as Ram Singh Dhesy of Savi Dharti and Gurminder Singh Thind who have planted hundreds of native species of trees."

I am reminded of references to Bhagat Puran Singh's attempts to alert people to environmental dangers and of Surjeet Kaur Chahal's work discussing ecology, particularly genetic engineering, from a Sikh perspective. Pardeep Singh also draws much inspiration from the Sikh Gurus themselves, who devised practical strategies to promote the welfare of the environment: "The seventh Guru, Guru Har Rai, for example, ran a herbal treatment center in Kiratpur, Panjab, which is now being revived with fresh plantation with the help of forest authorities. He also ran an animal clinic and used to arrange to collect sick animals for treatment to be re-released to the wild." A painting also comes to my mind of the fifth Guru, depicting his work at a center, not far from Amritsar [the holiest location to Sikhs], which he opened to treat and care for those suffering from leprosy.

Born in Malaysia, Pardeep Singh spent part of his childhood in the Panjab, which unleashed his fascination for the age-old relationship Panjabis have had with their natural surroundings. "There is a well-known Panjabi proverb which shows this love of nature," remarks Pardeep, "God sleeps in the tree, dreams in the animals, and wakes in man." His stay also brought to life the imagery from nature which permeates the compositions of Gurbani. He gives the example of "Barah Maah," the "Twelve Months," which evoke the changing seasons to explore the evolving state of the human being seeking union with her Creator:

> In this way, we come to see ourselves bound in both a physical and metaphysical relationship with the phenomena of nature. This has a far-reaching impact on how we understand the process of ethical-decision making. In our pre-

sent-day secular society, the individual person is viewed as having autonomy in such matters. Traditionally in Sikh culture, the person is viewed as a combination of mind, soul and body in the context of family, culture, environment, and nature. Thus, he or she is seen not as autonomous but rather as intimately integrated with extended family, community, and the natural world. This suggests we need a holistic approach to ethical and environmental matters. Sadly, many Sikhs today appear to be indifferent and unresponsive to the degradation of the environment in Panjab and our planet Earth. This is a disservice to Sikhism and humankind!

I picture some of the occasional sightings I've had of elderly, green-fingered Sikhs who visit their allotments on the edge of the Sandwell Valley, near where I live in Birmingham, England, and the touching scene of one such grandfather helping a young child to pat down some soil around a newly-bedded plant. My husband and I both share memories of our grandmothers, whose love for the earth has passed into family folklore. One was famed for growing strawberries in winter, such was her tender loving care and gardener's intuition; another would be found drying melon seeds or tangerine skins in the sun, ready for some home remedy or beauty preparation. Like most grandparents of their generation, they had the habit of being economical and efficient with resources, minimizing waste, and recycling.

Today in an average Sikh family setting, as well as a linguistic gulf separating elders from youngsters there is no doubt one of lifestyle and the attitudes which underpin our interaction with environment. Any initial shock elders may have felt at what goes into the garbage bin, the time that is spent in front of the TV, or the waste of food at large-scale family functions, has probably dulled over time to quiet tolerance. In some families, however, traditions which maintain a strong consciousness of gratitude and respect have filtered through, for example, in the tradition of covering one's head and meditatively chanting whilst preparing a meal, saying a short prayer before and after eating, and ensuring minimum wastage. An article from the SikhNet website explores this concept of a "conscious kitchen" with a host of practical ideas for Sikhs to "green" their daily habits.

London-based Pardeep Singh dedicates himself to a range of ecological initiatives both locally and nationally in the United Kingdom, with an intricate knowledge of the biodiversity to be found across a range of contexts. He also designs gardens, incorporating his concerns for sustainability, maintaining a holistic approach, and drawing out a sacred dimension. He continues to channel energy towards the Sikh community specifically, compiling reports such as "The Green Action Guide for London's Gurdwaras," "The Gurdwara as an Environmental Sanctuary," and "Healthy Eating for the Sangat" [Sikh community]. Changing community habits, he admits, is a slow and uphill struggle. To further this work, he helped to launch recently, the Sikh Environmental Network.

Other environmental work being done by Sikhs in the United Kingdom includes that of Parminder Garcha, who has helped to set up a community garden in Birmingham with the aid of a local Sikh women's group. Khalsa Wood, a project based within Bestwood Country Park on the northern urban fringe of Nottingham, engages local Sikhs in restoring the park. Non-Panjabi Sikhs, many of whom were inspired by Harbhajan Singh Yogi, are probably in the vanguard of Sikhs actively promoting healthy lifestyles with an environmental conscience. Some, such as the French-born Sikh couple who founded Aquarius Health in Cyprus, made a decision to move away from city life in West London and work towards establishing an eco-friendly health center closer to nature. Another French-born Sikh, Darshan Singh Rudel, who embraced the faith through personal encounter with practitioners of the tradition, now runs Raza organic farms in the Panjab. Some of my Panjabi Sikh relatives are now establishing a life closer to nature in the British countryside and making plans for a well-being center and a family-scale gurdwara.

None of those mentioned here are representative of Sikhs in Britain, any more than Monty Don, the BBC's organic gardener, is representative of the "British" and their lifestyle. They do, however, provide examples of individuals whose enterprises draw very consciously upon Sikh spiritual and cultural heritage, whose character is linked to the land and traditions of rural Panjab. Sikh teachings are emphatic that religion is not to be a form of escapism from the world, but a way of reconnecting with it. Those who take the decision to move from city to country seem to be driven by a hope of creating new models for living and increasing self-sufficiency in order to survive some of the problems which may befall us with a possible scarcity of resources in the future. In the meantime, other Sikh organizations, like the Nishkam Civic Centre in Birmingham, are working to foster greater well-being, cohesion, educational nurture, and social care within the environment of the city, with the idea that, once you help to generate understanding and peace within the human mind, greater and more sustainable peace is possible within society.

"Guru Nanak teaches me that the reality humans have created around themselves is a reflection of their inner state," concludes Pardeep. "The current instability of the natural system of the earth, the external environment of human beings, is only a reflection of the instability and pain within humans. The increasing barrenness of the earth's terrain is a reflection of the emptiness within the human soul."

How might this barrenness be overcome? The closing message of the *Guru Granth Sahib*, the sacred volume of scripture revered by Sikhs as a "living Guru," offers an answer:

Nanak, nam milai ta(n) jiva(n), tan man theevai haria.
"Says Nanak, by receiving the blessing of *nam,* the divine name of God-consciousness, I begin to truly live, and mind and body blossom forth in radiant greenery."

Introduction to article by S. Lourdunathan

In this article, Prof. Lourdunathan asserts that the current environmental crisis is due to human immorality and that this unhealthy and unwise behavior is prompted by particular ways of looking at the world of nature. These two dangerous ways of looking at the physical world are dualism and otherworldliness: Dualism maintains that the material world or the physical body is inferior, at the least, and unreal, at the most. Otherworldliness stresses a focus on the spiritual lying beyond us and an intentional ignoring of the immediate world at-hand.

By contrast, Sikhism's perspective appreciates and accents that God dwells in nature as its Creator and continuing Creator. Because God is immanent in the world, nature has intrinsic value and ought not to be treated as an object whose worth lies solely in what it can provide to satisfy human greed.

Prof. Lourdunathan names this better and healthier way of looking at the world of nature, "ecosophia," a term which denotes the wisdom required to promote sustainable ecology. Ecosophia can move humans beyond anthropocentrism (human-centeredness), he claims, to "holistic consciousness" (and conservation). No longer selfish, consumeristic, and antagonistic toward nature, we humans can then become more concerned with conservation. We can see the earth as "divine."

Ecosophical Concerns in the Sikh Tradition

S. Lourdunathan

The contemporary transnational capitalist-technocratic society, with its profit interests which claim to have mastered the techniques of controlling and conquering Nature, is, unfortunately, faced with the problems of environmental degradation, a basic threat to global living.

The egoistic human potency to corrupt and pollute has eroded the phase of nature, while Nature has all along been nourishing, protecting, sheltering, life-giving, creative and maternal. Nature, earth, its biosphere and atmosphere have been mortally wounded, due to the immorality of man. The life-giving mother earth *(terra mater)* is turned to be life-destroying, to the extent of self-annihilation. The scientific community partially describes this crisis-situation as deforestation, depletion of ozone layer, global warming, impoverishment, etc.

However, this factual description is only one side of the coin, i.e., the technological. The reasons for this crisis are many. They include factors such as racial discrimination, economic exploitation, caste-ism, world-wars, socio-political colonization, cultural invasions, religious fundamentalism, and so on. Hence, the reasons for the crisis are not merely scientific and technological, but also non-scientific. In other words, the ecological problem is multi-faceted.

Deep down, the radicality (root cause) of the crisis is, philosophical (ideological). It is philosophical in the sense that the worldviews (perspectives or the ways of looking at) of those who are responsible for the destruction of Nature often tend to be partial (monolithic), dualistic, and non-earthly (other worldly); for instance, the idealism of Plato denying the reality of the World, affirms only the Archetype, and hence it is partial, not ecological.

Naive realism and materialism assert that the cosmos is what ranks first, and consciousness is only secondary (one-sided); existentialists, like Sartre, affirm the world and consciousness as primary, and confuse the real cosmos with the human-world alone. In the Indian philosophical tradition, *Vedanta,* for example, affirms the primacy of the ideal of the "identity of atman or Brahman," to the extent of giving only a relative or no importance to the existence of the world (*maya* theory).

The frontier-mentality of human-centricism (humanism) of the 18th century proved to be not sufficiently human, as it implied the development of the dominant class and the Western scientific man's interests. These are some of the instances to point out the fact that our worldviews that shape human attitude to life and Nature were predominantly partial and other-worldly, implying an inbuilt insensitivity to ecology.

Given this context of the metaphysical exclusion of Nature, it is high time that we search for philosophical foundations that are eco-relational. It is the moral responsibility of man to establish a new humanism without "human-centricism" of the West. In other words, the practical relationship of man with Nature must be redefined or deconstructed, outside the "wrong kinds of philosophizing."

Perhaps one of the ways of responding to the situation is to investigate the philosophical foundations of the South Asian ethos, and that, too, of those who are neither monolithic nor other-worldly. In contrast to European individualism, the remarkable characteristic of West Asian Religious ethos (that of Buddhism, Taoism, Confucianism, etc.) is holistic—these religions are in general anti-individualistic, not consumeristic and indiscriminative. The spirit of peace, justice, global living, harmony with Nature, is foundational to these religions.

This study is a tentative endeavor to reconstruct the ecological wisdom embedded in the Sikh tradition as a viable response to global living in the context of the environmental crisis, for if the ecological crisis is defined as the alienation/estrangement of human life from Mother Nature, it is the responsibility of humans to establish again filial relationship with Her, which in turn will develop into a certain subjective, emotional attitude towards Nature.

What is Ecosophia? How and in what sense may Sikhism, as a religion, be considered ecosophical? Does the Sikh scriptural tradition (*Sri Guru Granth Sahib*) have the potential to promote deep ecological consciousness? These are some of the inter-related queries that I will try to expound.

The objective will then be to highlight the Sikh emotional-religious-spiritual and the philosophical attachment with Mother Nature. Such an attempt is in fact a prerequisite to breaking away the egoistic, antagonistic, consumeristic attitude, relationship of man with Nature. In other words, it is to interpretatively understand the Sikh tradition in the context of promoting peace, justice, ecology— even though strictly speaking, attempts of this kind may not directly or factually offer a praxis [action] or theory to the global crisis.

Human attitude to religion may be classified into three kinds: First, the fundamentalists. Second, those who deny everything of religion, with a view that religion is redundant and hence it has no positive role to play in society. Third are those who develop empathy to religion in general, and continue to maintain a religious outlook which goes beyond any sectarianism. They are those who strive for the formation of alternative frames that would actively respond to the emerging problems of human society. They are of liberal nature, organically interested in the authenticity of their religion.

The third, namely the attitude of the liberal, is adapted to respond to the ecological crisis, since it allows the advocacy for searching into newer and meaningful ways concerning one's religion that contribute to the problem situation. Such an approach brings the religionists and the non-religionists together in harmony—and, in fact, provides the common, universal theoretical foundation for inter- and extra-religious encounters. With this view, may I be allowed to strike a liberal attitude to Sikhism.

Ecosophia in Sikhism

The term ecosophia literally means the wisdom of the Universe that is required for the promotion of sustainable and peaceful ecology. The combination of the two Greek words, *Oikos + Sophos*, gives rise to Ecosophia (*Oikos* means the Cosmos, the household of being). Ecosophia is a philosophy of ecological harmony and equilibrium. It is the kind of wisdom (sophia) that is suggestive of norms, ways of perceiving Nature, as against dominant world-views. It is an attempt to go beyond anthropocentrism towards holistic consciousness of the universe. It is a new mediation of humanity and society with Nature. It involves developing a certain religious attitude towards nature-eco-spirituality. It views that social and environmental problems are the consequence of specific social relations of dominations.

Within this frame, ecology (mere environmentalism) is elevated from a scientific description to philosophy, in this sense, it is called deep ecology. It is to view that the problems of human society are not to be treated in isolation with other social systems and norms, for "systems are integrated wholes, whose properties cannot be reduced to those of its parts."

Ecosophia is the articulation of religious and philosophical world-views that provide a "face-to-face relation with Nature."

The ecosophical paradigm aims at the liberation of life, and that necessarily includes the liberation of Nature, women and the underprivileged. It is an attempt to contact with the intrinsic dignity/worth of Nature, women and the downtrodden. It aims to establish relations in justice. Cosmic unity and biocentric equality are the two ultimate norms of ecosophia. Ecosophism essentially recognizes that both human and non-human life on earth has intrinsic values. It abnegates any form of domination and subjugation. People and Nature are the core of ecosophia(ism).

The issue now is to ascertain whether Sikhism is ecosophical. This question may be responded to by delving into the metaphysical foundations of Sikhism, and its Scripture—*Sri Guru Granth Sahib*—for that which is essential of a religion is its scripture, and that which is central to the scripture is its metaphysical foundations.

The Idea of God: Eco-Spirituality

Apart from the transcendental idea of God, Sikhism lays emphasis on the immanent nature of God. God, for Sikhism, is a "Living Truth," the Creator and the Sustainer of the Universe. He is *ik-oan-kar,* meaning that God manifests Himself as a determinated Infinity in the dimension of Time and History. He is the manifesting material Reality. He is conceived to be the Creator-Person *(karta-purakhu).* He is immanent in the cosmic form *(moorati).* The act of creation by God, for Sikhism, is a never-ending process; He is the continuous life-giving principle. He creates, animates, and sustains Nature. Nature is the dwelling place of God, and hence reverence to Nature is a must. *SGGS [Sri Guru Granth Sahib*—the scriptures of the Sikh tradition] reads:

> He, the Creator, Himself creates the world . . . and watches all. . . . He alone imparts understanding (*SGGS*: p.767).

Where is this Creator-God?

The Lord (it is said) is contained in spaces and inter-spaces. He cherishes all beings (*SGGS*: p.760). The Lord has made this world an arena of symphonic dance. Creating the entire creation, He has placed in it various forms and colors (*SGGS*: p.746). The Lord abides amongst all (*SGGS*: p.748). The devotee remains pleased with their Lord and sees Him, in water, land, nether regions, and firmament (*SGGS*: p.748). God who has created, sustains the creation; He gives sustenance to all. . . . [He is] thine Benefactor (*SGGS*: p.751).

There are innumerable texts that reflect the mind of Sikhism, that God is the source of cosmic formation, and He manifests in it, and hence, Nature is not a mere object that could be utilized to human ends—but it has intrinsic dignity and value.

The Cause for Ecological Imbalance

The human mind, by being self-conceited, loses communion with Nature, and ultimately with God. This causes him misery and it is the repeated assertion of Sikhism: The thief of self-conceit (domination) is robbing the house *(oikos).* . . now he finds no place to rest (*SGGS*: p. 752). By affirming the immanence of God and His presence in the Creation, the Sikh religion imparts the spirit of self-righteousness to the entire subject of Nature.

The Idea of World

In contrast to philosophies that encourage world-denial, the Sikh tradition affirms the reality/authenticity of the world/body. Body is the mediation to the attainment of the Lord. The earth and the "here and now" is the space for liberation of life: Engrossing into duality leads to forgetfulness of the dwelling God

(*SGGS*: p.757). In the body are the invaluable wealth and the brimful treasures of Lord's mediation. . . . Within the body abide all, the continents, the worlds, and the nether regions. In the body dwells the Beneficent Lord, the life of the world Who cherishes all. Ever illustrated is the body-bride . . . it meditates on the Name (*SGGS*: p.754).

Thus, in Sikhism, body symbolically stands for earth, Nature, Cosmos; through her (bridegroom), attainment of the Lord (peace) is possible. In the ecosophical language, the Sikh religion with its affirmation of the earth as Divine, calls for continuous consciousness of its harmony and unity. The earth cannot be consumed for selfish purposes, but conserved—on the basis of need and not greed.

The Earth as Dharmasal [*Dharmasal* or *Dharmasala* is literally a "place or seat of religion;" it was the precursor to the *Gurdwara*, a Sikh place of worship and community center. However, in Sikh theology, all of the earth is regarded as *Dharmasal*, a place for practicing religious duty.]

Amidst (creation) He fixed the earth, a place for righteous action (Japuji: *SGGS*-7). According to Sikh belief, the world is Holy, and one's relation to it must also be holy. The whole world is Holy. Be you in its purity absorbed. By discarding egoism does one find acceptance at God's portal (*SGGS*: p.142). By this portrayal of the world (earth) as a place for righteousness and purity, Guru Nanak insists that we relate with others with equality and justice, and that there is a possibility of a future for the history of Nature, for it has a spiritual meaning. The monistic denial of the "reality" of the world, for the Sikh religious mind, is inadequate and un-Godly . . . .

It is up to the Sikh community to reflect and live its ecological truth claims, for they believe that truth is high, but higher still is truthful living.

Introduction to article by Mary Evelyn Tucker

In this article, professor of Chinese religions Mary Evelyn Tucker seconds the insight of Thomas Berry that an awareness of world religions will be necessary in order to reinvigorate the human spirit to work toward solving ecological crises. In this regard, she points out that East Asian religions have much to offer.

Taoism (Daoism) recognizes the closeness of humans to nature and the need to live harmoniously with the natural world. Taking a more passive approach, Daoism's ideal is the hermit, who withdraws in order to live in-tune with the *Tao* (nature's Way). For Taoists, the human-earth relationship is primary.

Confucianism recognizes the importance of human relationships and the need to live in an orderly society in harmony with nature. Taking a more active approach, Confucianism's ideal is the sage or teacher who acts in the world in ways that are empathic to a series of concentric circles beginning with the individual and reaching out to the entire cosmos. For Confucianists, the individual-society-nature relationship is primary.

Tucker concludes that a combination of both traditions is necessary to be fruitful in dealing with our environmental problems: Taoism's advocacy of non-interference (*wu-wei*) with nature, regarding it as valued for its own sake (intrinsic worth), and seeking harmony with it rather than control over it, joined with Confucianism's emphasis on actions which maintain proper and healthy relationships with all personal connections, indicate that nature is not a resource to exploit, but rather a community to appreciate and respect.

Ecological Themes in Taoism and Confucianism

Mary Evelyn Tucker

Humans do not oppose Earth and therefore can comfort all things, for their standard is the Earth. Earth does not oppose Heaven and therefore can sustain all things, for its standard is Heaven. Heaven does not oppose Tao and therefore can cover all things, for its standard is Tao. Tao does not oppose Nature and therefore it attains its character of being. (a Taoist commentary from Wang Pi, 226-249 C.E.)

Mencius answered [King Hui], "If your majesty can practice human government to the people, reduce punishments and fines, lower taxes and levies, make it possible for the fields to be plowed deep and the weeding well done, men of strong body, in their days of leisure, may cultivate their filial piety, brotherly respect, loyalty, and faithfulness, thereby serving their fathers and elder brothers at home and their elders and superiors abroad." (a Confucian text from Mencius, 372-289 B.C.E.)

Over two decades ago, [cultural anthropologist] Thomas Berry called for "creating a new consciousness of the multiform religious traditions of humankind" as a means toward renewal of the human spirit in addressing the urgent problems of contemporary society. More recently, Tu Wei-ming has written of the need to go "beyond the Enlightenment mentality" in exploring the spiritual resources of the global community to meet the challenge of the ecological crisis.

In drawing upon the great religious traditions of the past for a new ecological orientation in the present, it is clear that the traditions of East Asia have much to offer. My method here is to examine some of the principal texts of Taoism and Confucianism for a phenomenological description of ecological worldviews embedded in these traditions. I risk the inevitable distortions of reducing complex teachings from 2500-year-old traditions to generalizations that need qualification and development. I am also relying primarily on the philosophical and religious ideas of these traditions as evident in their texts and am not discussing their varied religious practices which arose in different periods of Chinese history. Nor am I making claims for a historical consciousness in China of the issues of ecology as we . . . understand them. Furthermore, I am aware of the ever-present gap between theoretical positions and practical applications in dealing with the environment throughout history. I am also conscious of the dark side of each religious tradition as it developed in particular historical contexts. Nonetheless, in seeking guidance from the past it is becoming increasingly important to examine the perspectives of earlier civilizations and their attitudes toward nature as we seek more comprehensive worldviews and environmental ethics in the present. There is not sufficient time or space to work out all of these methodological issues here. However, I would suggest that this project is an important step in creating a new ecumenism of the multiform religious traditions of the human community in dialogue with pressing contemporary problems such as the environment and social justice.

General Comments on Taoism and Confucianism

The two indigenous traditions of China, Taoism and Confucianism, arose in the so-called Axial Age in the first millennium before the birth of Christ. As Karl Jaspers [German psychiatrist and philosopher who died in 1969] noted, this was approximately the same time as the philosophers in Greece, the prophets in Israel, Zoroaster in Persia, and Buddha in India. In China, this period in the Chou dynasty was a time of great intellectual creativity known as the 100 philosophers.

Although there are many historical uncertainties and ongoing scholarly debates about the life and the writings of Lao-tzu and Confucius, it is indisputable that these two figures are of primary importance in Chinese religion and philosophy. Indeed, some writers on Chinese thought see these traditions as complementary to each other and in a kind of creative tension. While Taoism and Confucianism are quite different in their respective teachings, they share a worldview that might be described as organic, vitalistic, and holistic. They see the universe as a dynamic, ongoing process of continual transformation. The creativity and unity of the cosmos are constant themes which appear in the Taoist and Confucianist texts. The human has a special role in this vitalistic universe. This is viewed in a more passive manner by the Taoists and a more active mode by the Confucians.

It is, however, this organic, vitalistic worldview which has special relevance for developing a contemporary ecological perspective. Indeed, it can be said that within this holistic view Taoist and Confucian thought might provide an important balance of passive and active models for ecological theory and practice. Like a *yin-yang* circle of complementary opposites, Taoist and Confucian thinkers have evoked important considerations from each other and may still do the same for us today.

In very general terms, we can compare and contrast these two traditions as follows. Taoism emphasizes primary causality as resting in the *Tao*, while Confucianism stresses the importance of secondary causality in the activities of human beings. Thus, the principal concern in Taoism is for harmony with the *Tao*, the nameless Way which is the source of all existence. In Confucianism, the stress is on how humans can live together and create a just society with a benevolent government. For both the Taoists and the Confucians, harmony with nature is important. The Taoists emphasize the primacy of unmediated closeness to nature to encourage simplicity and spontaneity in individuals and in human relations. For the Taoists, developing techniques of meditation is critical. The Confucians, especially the Neo-Confucians, stress harmonizing with the changing patterns in nature so as to adapt human action and human society appropriately to nature's deeper rhythms. For them the *Book of Changes* is an important means of establishing balance with nature and with other humans.

For the Taoists, in order to be in consonance with the Tao in nature, one must withdraw from active involvement in social and political affairs and learn how to preserve and nourish nature and human life. For the Confucians, social and political commitment was an indispensable part of human responsibility to create an orderly society in harmony with nature. Indeed, for the Confucians, cultivating oneself morally and intellectually was a means of establishing a peaceful and productive society. The ideal for the Taoist, then, was the hermit in a mountain retreat, while for the Confucian it was the sage, the teacher, and the civil servant in the midst of affairs of government and education. Taoism did provide a model of an ideal ruler, but one who led without overt involvement but rather by subtle indirection and detachment. The Confucians, on the other hand, called for a moral ruler who would be like a pole star for the people, practicing humane government for the benefit of all. The Taoist stressed the principle of non-egocentric action (*wu-wei*) in harmony with nature for both ruler and followers. The Confucians, on the other hand, underscored the importance of human action for the betterment of society by the ruler, ministers, teachers, and ordinary citizens. A pristine innocence and spontaneity were valued by the Taoists, while the Confucians continually emphasized humanistic education and ethical practice for the improvement of individuals and society as a whole.

It is perhaps some combination of these two perspectives which may be fruitful for our own thinking today. In order to understand and respect natural processes, we need a greater Taoist attention to the subtle unfolding of the principles and processes of nature. As the deep ecologists constantly remind us, without this fine attunement to the complexities of nature and to ourselves as one species among many others, we may continue to contribute unwittingly to destructive environmental practices. Yet without the Confucian understanding of the importance of moral leadership, an emphasis on education, and a sense of human responsibility to a larger community of life, we may lose the opportunity to change the current pattern of assault on the natural world. Taoism challenges us to radically reexamine human-earth relations, while Confucianism calls us to rethink the profound interconnection of individual-society-nature. Let us turn to examine the worldview of each of these traditions and their potential contributions to environmental ethics.

Taoism and Ecology: Cosmology and Ethics

The principle text of Taoism is the *Tao te Ching* (The Way and Its Power), also known by the title *Lao Tzu*, its author. There have been numerous translations of this text into many languages and perhaps no other Chinese work compares to it in terms of international popularity. The *Tao te Ching* contains a cosmology and an ethics which may have some relevance in our contemporary discussions on ecology.

In terms of cosmology, the Tao refers to the unmanifest source of all life which is eternal and ineffable yet fecund and creative. "The Nameless is the origin of Heaven and Earth; the named is the mother of all things." The *Tao*, then, is the self-existent source of all things, namely, a primary cause. It is both a power which generates and a process which sustains. It is the unity behind the multiplicity of the manifest world. It is beyond distinction or name and can only be approached through image, paradox, or intuition. In its manifest form in the phenomenal world, it is said to have no particular characteristics and thus be empty. As such it is full of potentiality. Indeed, the "*Tao* is empty (like a bowl); it may be used but its capacity is never exhausted." It can be described, however, with images such as valley, womb, and vessel, suggestive of receptivity and productivity.

The implications of this holistic cosmology for an environmental ethic should be somewhat self-evident. There is a distinct emphasis in Taoist thought on valuing nature for its own sake, not for utilitarian ends. The natural world is not a resource to exploit, but a complex of dynamic life processes to appreciate and respect. Harmony with nature, rather than control, is the ultimate Taoist goal. This tradition has certain affinities with contemporary movements in deep ecology which decry an overly anthropocentric position of human dominance over nature. Indeed, the Taoists, like the deep ecologists, would say that manipulation of nature will lead to counterproductive results.

To achieve harmony with nature, the Taoists value simplicity and spontaneity. They distrust education and the imposition of moral standards as interfering with true naturalness. Intuitive knowledge and a pristine innocence are highly regarded. A direct, unmediated encounter with nature is far better than book knowledge or hypocritical morality. As Lao-tzu urges, one should "Abandon sageliness and discard wisdom; then the people will benefit a hundredfold . . . Manifest plainness, embrace simplicity, reduce selfishness, have few desires."

Moreover, in terms of human action, that which is understated, not forceful or directive, is considered optimal. Excess, extravagance, and arrogance are to be avoided. Non-egocentric action (*wu-wei*) which is free from desire and attachments is essential. In short, "by acting without action, all things will be in order." In light of this, the *Tao te Ching* celebrates the paradox that yielding brings strength, passivity creates power, death creates new life.

These ideas are illustrated in the text with feminine images of fecundity and strength springing from openness and receptivity such as in motherhood, in an empty vessel, or in a valley. They also underlie images such as water wearing away at solid rock or the idea of an uncarved block waiting to reveal its form at the hands of a skilled sculptor. These demonstrate the potentiality and generative power which exist in unexpected and hidden places.

> He who knows the male (active force) and keeps to the
> female (the passive force or receptive element)
> becomes the ravine of the world.
>
> He will never part from eternal virtue.
> He who knows glory but keeps to humility,
> becomes the valley of the world.
>
> He will be proficient in eternal virtue,
> and returns to the state of simplicity (uncarved wood).

In short, the *Tao te Ching* demonstrates the ultimate paradox of the coincidence of opposites, namely, that yielding is a form of strength. (This is clearly illustrated in the martial art of Judo, which means the "way of yielding.") Indeed, the lesson of Taoism is that reversal is the movement of the *Tao*, for many things easily turn into their opposites. "Reversion is the action of *Tao*. Weakness is the function of *Tao*. All things in the world come from being. And being comes from non-being."

Thus, both personally and politically Taoism calls for non-interfering action. A Taoist government would be one of conscious detachment and the ideal leader would be one who governs least. While this seems antithetical to the Confucian notion of active political involvement, the wisdom of the Taoist ideal of noninterference was not lost in the highest quarters of Chinese Confucian government. Over one of the thrones in the imperial palace in Beijing are the characters for *wu-wei* (non-egocentric action), perhaps serving as a reminder of the importance of a detached attitude in political affairs.

All of this has enormous implications for our interactions with nature, namely that humans cannot arrogantly or blindly force nature into our mold. To cooperate with nature in a Taoist manner requires a better understanding of an appreciation for nature's processes. While an extreme Taoist position might advocate complete noninterference with nature, a more moderate Taoist approach would call for interaction with nature in a far less exploitive manner. Such cooperation with nature would sanction the use of appropriate or intermediate technology when necessary and would favor the use of the organic fertilizers and natural farming methods. In terms of economic policy, it would foster limited growth within a steady state economy that could support sustainable not exploitative development. Clearly, a Taoist ecological position is one with significant potential in the contemporary world.

Confucianism and Ecology: Cosmology and Ethics

Let us turn to the early classical texts of the *Analects* and the *Mencius* to explore the ecological dimensions of Confucian thought. These works have had an enormous impact on Chinese society, education, and government for over two millennia. Along with two shorter texts, the *Great Learning* and the *Doctrine of the Mean*, these became known as the *Four Books* and were the basis of the civil service examination system from the fourteenth century until the twentieth.

Cosmologically, early Confucianism, like Taoism, understood the world to be part of a changing, dynamic and unfolding universe. The ongoing and unfolding process of nature was affirmed by the Confucians, and seasonal harmony was highly valued. There is no common creation myth *per se* for the Confucians or Taoists. Rather, the universe is seen as self-generating, guided by the unfolding of the *Tao*, a term the Confucians shared with Taoists although with variations on its meaning in different contexts and periods. There is no personification of evil; instead, there is a balance of opposite forces in the concept of the *yin* and the *yang*.

Indeed, there is no radical split between transcendence and immanence such as occurs in the Western religions. In fact, it has become widely accepted that the sense of immanence rather than transcendence dominates both Taoist and Confucian thought. Although this needs qualification, it is true that the notion of "the secular as the sacred" was critical in Chinese philosophy and religion. The significance of this view is that a balance of the natural and the human worlds was essential in both Taoist and Confucian thought (While the Taoists emphasized harmony with nature and downplayed human action, the Confucians stressed the importance of human action and the critical role of social and political institutions.)

Within this cosmology, certain ethical patterns emerged in Confucianism which are distinct from Taoism. Examining these patterns may be helpful for our understanding of the ecological dimensions of Confucian thought. While Taoism can be characterized as a naturalistic ecology having certain affinities with contemporary deep ecology, Confucianism might be seen as a former social ecology having some similarities with the contemporary movement of the same name. Taoism is clearly nature centered, while Confucianism tends to be more human centered. Neither tradition, however, succumbs to the problem of egocentric anthropocentrism or radical individualism such as has been characteristic of certain movements in the modern West. Both have a profound sense of the importance of nature as primary. For the Taoists, nature is the basis of nourishing individual life and for the Confucians, it is indispensable for sustaining communal life.

A Confucian ethic might be described as a form of social ecology because a key component is relationality in the human order against the background of the natural order. A profound sense of the interconnectedness of the human with one another and with nature is central to Confucian thinking. The individual is never seen as an isolated entity, but always as a person in relation to another and to the cosmos. A useful image for describing the Confucian ethical system is a series of concentric circles with the person in the center. In the circle closest to the individual is one's family, then one's teachers, one's friends, the government, and in the outer circle is the universe itself. In the Confucian system, relationality extends from the individual in the family outward to the cosmos. This worldview has been described as an anthropocosmic one, embracing heaven, earth, and human as an interactive whole. In Confucianism, from the time of the early classical text of the *Book of History*, heaven and earth have been called the great parents who have provided life and sustenance. Just as parents in the family deserve filial respect, so do heaven and earth. Indeed, we are told they should not be exploited wantonly by humans.

In Confucianism, then, the individual is both supported by and supportive of those in the other circles which surround him or her. The exchange of mutual obligations and responsibilities between the individual, others in the these circles, and the cosmos itself constitute the relational basis of Confucian societies. Like a social glue, the give and take of these relationships help to give shape and character to these societies. Many of these patterns of social and cosmological exchanges become embedded in rituals which constitute the means of expressing reciprocal relations between people and with nature. Thus, the value of mutual reciprocity and of belonging to a series of groups is fostered in Confucian societies. In all of this, education was critical. As the *Great Learning (Ta Hsueh)* so clearly demonstrates, to establish peace under heaven we must begin with the cultivation of the mind-and-heart of the person. Education for the Confucians embraced the moral and intellectual dimensions of a person and was intended to prepare them to be a fully contributing citizen of the larger society.

In addition to these ethical guidelines of social ecology for the individual in relation to others and to the cosmos itself, Confucianism developed an elaborate theory of government which might be described as a political ecology. Taking the same model of the individual embedded in a series of concentric circles, the Confucians situated the emperor at the center and suggested that his moral example would have a rippling effect outward like a pebble dropped into a pond. The influence of this morality would be felt by all the people, and human government would be possible when the emperor had compassion on the people and established appropriate economic, social, and ecological policies.

Thus, while both Confucianism and Taoism are relational in their overall orientation, Confucianism is clearly more activist, especially with regard to moral leadership and practical policies. Many of the principles of humane government such as those advocated by Mencius and other Confucians include policies such as an ecological sensitivity to land and other resources, equitable distribution of goods and services, fair taxation, and allowing the people to enjoy nature and cultivate human relations. The recognition that humane government rests on sustainable agriculture and maintaining a balance with nature is key to all Confucian political thought.

Thus, both in terms of individuals and society as a whole, there was a concern for larger relationships that would lead toward harmony of people with one another and with nature, which supported them. This social and political ecology within an anthropocosmic worldview has something to offer in our own period of rampant individualism, self-interested government, and exploitation of natural resources. The continuation of cooperative group effort to achieve common goals that are for the benefit of the whole society is an important model for a new form of social ecology. At the same time, the ideal of humane government which develops and distributes resources equitably is central to a political ecology so much needed at the present.

Conclusion

This study only begins to suggest some of the rich resources available in the traditions of Taoism and Confucianism for formulating an ecological cosmology and an environmental ethics in our time. As we seek a new balance in human-earth relations, it is clear that the perspectives from other religious and philosophical traditions may be instrumental in formulating new ways of thinking and acting more appropriately to both the vast rhythms and the inevitable limitations of nature. As our worldview in relation to nature is more clearly defined, we can hope that our actions will reflect both a Taoist appreciation for natural ecology and a Confucian commitment to social and political ecology.

List of Contributors

Paul Brockelman is University Professor of Religious Studies and Professor of Philosophy *Emeritus* at the University of New Hampshire.

Clifford Chalmers Cain is Professor of Religious Studies at Westminster College in Fulton, Missouri.

Christopher Key Chapple is the Navin and Pratima Doshi Professor of Indic and Comparative Theology at Loyola Marymount University in Los Angeles, California.

His Holiness the Fourteenth Dalai Lama is the spiritual and political leader in exile of the People of Tibet, Dharmsala, India.

Susan M. Darlington is Professor of Anthropology and Asian Studies at Hampshire College.

Eric M. Katz is a professor in the Department of Humanities and Social Sciences at the New Jersey Institute of Technology.

David Robert Kinsley was a member of the Religious Studies Department at McMaster University, Hamilton, Ontario, Canada, from 1969 until his death in 2000.

S. Lourdunathan is a philosopher at Arul Anandar College in Madurai, India.

Joel W. Martin is Chair of the Department of Religious Studies at the University of California at Riverside.

Seyyed Hossein Nasr is University Professor of Islamic Studies at George Washington University in Washington, D.C.

Iain Provan is a professor of Hebrew Bible (Old Testament) at Regent University in Vancouver, Canada.

Gopinder Kaur Sagoo is a post-graduate researcher at the School of Education, the University of Birmingham, England.

Chief Seattle was a tribal leader of the Puget Sound Indians in the Pacific Northwest.

Elizabeth Theokritoff is a member of the teaching faculty of the Institute for Orthodox Christian Studies in Cambridge, England.

Mary Evelyn Tucker is Senior Lecturer in Religion and the Environment at Yale University.

Index

Clifford Chalmers Cain. Photo by Gina Campagna.

About the Editor

CLIFFORD CHALMERS CAIN is Professor of Religious Studies at Westminster College in Fulton, Missouri. Cain holds two doctoral degrees and has written books and articles in the fields of contemporary theology, ecology, religion, and science.